BRIGHT IDEAS

More Christmas Art and Craft

D0542434

Compiled by Sue Loveridge

Published by Scholastic Publications Ltd,
Villiers House, Clarendon Avenue,
Leamington Spa, Warwickshire CV32 5PR.

© 1986 Scholastic Publications Ltd
Reprinted 1987, 1989, 1991

Ideas drawn from Scholastic magazines.

Compiled by Sue Loveridge
Edited by Philip Steele
Illustrations by Fred Haycock

Printed in Great Britain by
Loxley Brothers Ltd, Sheffield

ISBN 0-590-70601-2

Front cover: Crystal Forms, Oxford Scientific Films.
Back cover: Crystal Forms, Oxford Scientific Films.

Contents

Introduction

What have a German prune man, animal crackers, a collar of paper snowflakes and a tissue paper Christmas pudding got in common with a paper lantern?

The answer lies in this book. They are just a few of the Christmas art and craft ideas to be found, along with some old favourites such as embroidery cards and chains and streamers and some less familiar Christmas activities. The ideas cover a whole range of activities with chapters on: Christmas Cards; Tree Decorations; Room Decorations and Mobiles; Crackers and Table Decorations; Other Lands, Other Ages . . .; Party Hats and Fancy Dress; Christmas Gifts; and Christmas Plays and Pageants. The chapter on Techniques provides useful tips and the Templates and Designs given on pages 100–126, all of which can be photocopied, help make the book a ready source of ideas.

The ideas can be used as they are or as stepping stones. They can be elaborated upon or simplified, enlarged or reduced. Measurements have been kept to a minimum to allow plenty of scope for individual interpretation and development.

The age ranges given are meant only as general guidelines and should be regarded as flexible. The children's experience and expertise will often allow ideas to be adopted to suit. Likewise the group sizes given can be varied to suit your needs.

Most of the ideas use material that is readily available in the classroom or home, or which could be easily obtained, without incurring too much expense. All the ideas have been tried and tested; many have been drawn from articles published in Scholastic magazines.

More Bright Ideas for Christmas Art and Craft will be a valuable source of ideas for teachers, parents and children alike. There is a great deal of fun to be had from Christmas preparations and I hope this book will provide you with the information to make your Christmas a great success.

Sue Loveridge

Christmas cards

Christmas pud'

Age range
Five plus.

Group size
Individuals.

What you need
Card, tissue paper (white, black, brown), gummed paper (red, green), adhesive, scissors.

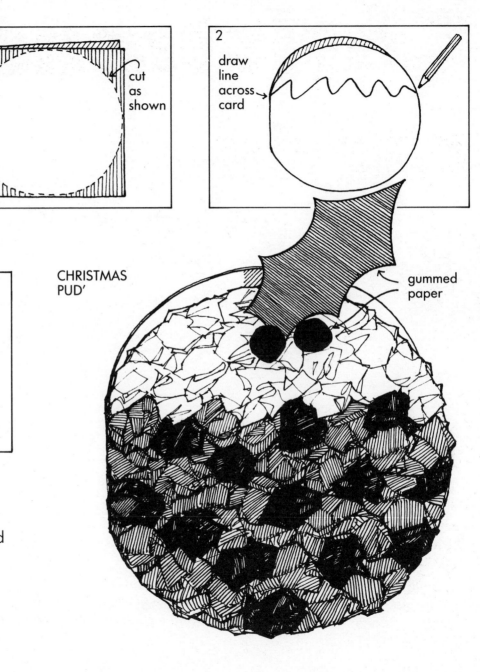

CHRISTMAS PUD'

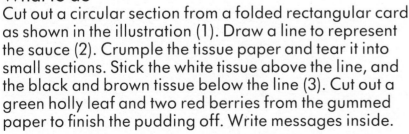

What to do
Cut out a circular section from a folded rectangular card as shown in the illustration (1). Draw a line to represent the sauce (2). Crumple the tissue paper and tear it into small sections. Stick the white tissue above the line, and the black and brown tissue below the line (3). Cut out a green holly leaf and two red berries from the gummed paper to finish the pudding off. Write messages inside.

Stand-up cards

Age range
Five plus.

Group size
Individuals.

What you need
Thin card, coloured paper, scissors, adhesive.

stick on

cut-out design

card base

What to do
Cut out a design: a snowman, perhaps, a Christmas tree or a stocking. Decorate it by sticking on coloured paper. The completed motif should then be stuck on to a rectangular card, folded as shown in the illustration, so that about one-third stands up above the fold.

Wax rubbings

Age range
Five plus.

Group size
Individuals or pairs.

What you need
Scraps of card, wax crayons, paper, masking tape, felt tips, gummed paper (especially gold or silver), mounting card, scissors.

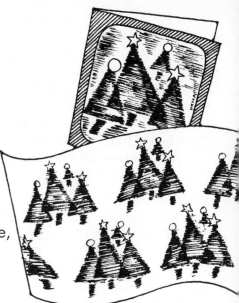

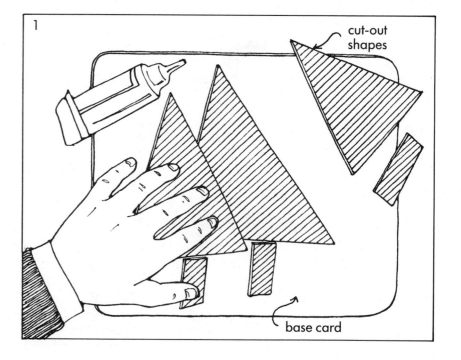

1

cut-out shapes

base card

What to do

Wax rubbings make excellent cards; the same principle may be used to decorate wrapping paper. Cut out scraps of card into bold shapes, and mount them on the base card (1). When they have dried, you are ready to take a rubbing. Find a piece of paper slightly larger than the base card: hold it firmly over the base, or use masking tape so that it does not move. Using the *side* of a wax crayon, rub carefully over the paper (2), so that an image of the relief surface is gradually revealed. Trim the rubbing and mount it on to a folded card. Further detail can be added to the rubbing with felt tips or gummed paper shapes (3).

To make wrapping paper, use the same technique. Move the wrapping paper around, so that the block is under a different area each time: in this way a pattern can be formed.

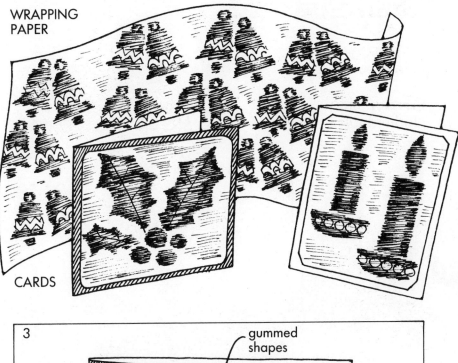

WRAPPING PAPER

CARDS

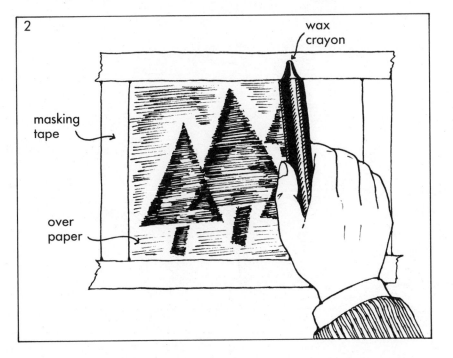

2

wax crayon

masking tape

over paper

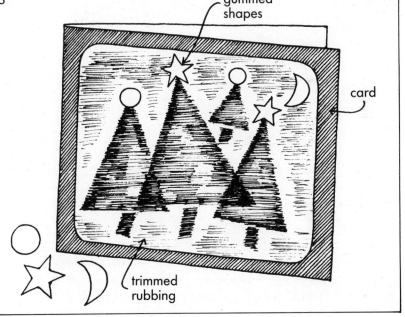

3

gummed shapes

card

trimmed rubbing

Embroidery

Designs on page 107

Age range
Five to six plus.

Group size
Individuals.

What you need
Squared paper,
suitable fabric,
thread or wool,
needles,
card.

What to do
This card design makes use of simple embroidery. Use squared paper to plan the motif, making its shape bold and simple. Some examples are given on page 107. The children should make up the design using cross stitch or even a running stitch. Fringe the edges of the fabric and attach to a piece of card as shown.

motif planned out on squared paper

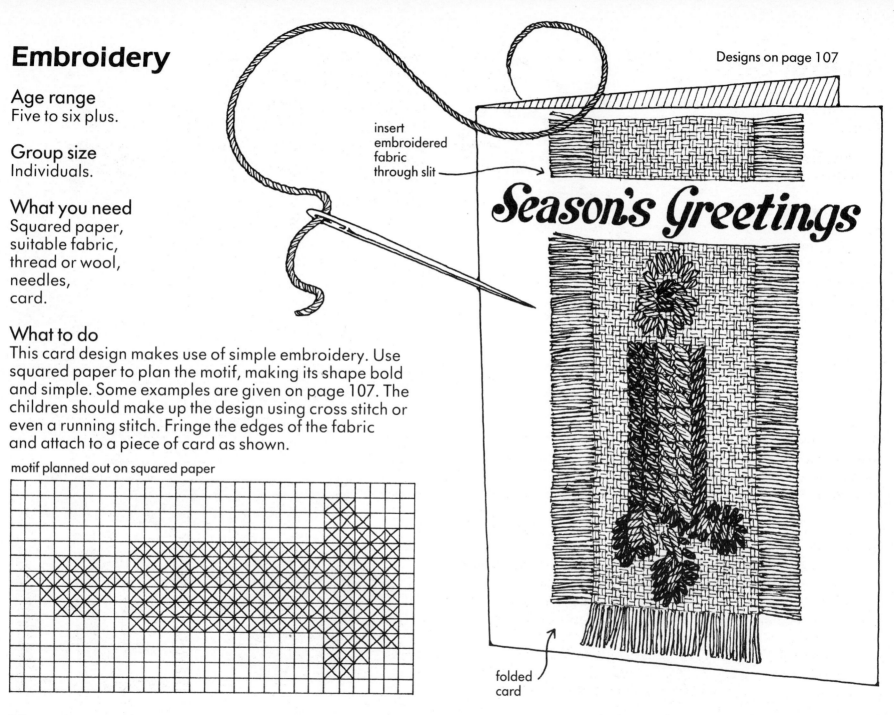

insert
embroidered
fabric
through slit

Season's Greetings

folded
card

10

Splatter cards

Age range
Six plus.

Group size
Individuals.

What you need
Scrap card
(for template or stencil),
scissors,
old toothbrush,
lollypop stick,
paint,
paper,
card,
felt tips or gummed paper,
glue.

Designs on pages 108–110

What to do
Cut out a stencil design (see page 108) from the scrap
card and lay it over the paper. Splatter on the paint with
an old toothbrush or lollypop stick. You will get a
coloured image in the shape of the window you have cut.

Alternatively, cut out a template and lay it on the paper.
Splatter on the paint; when you lift off the stencil, you will
be left with the paint surrounding a clear image.

Experiment with the two ways. Move the stencils so that
patterns overlap. Change the colours for complementary
patterns. When the paint is dry, further details can be
added with gummed paper or felt tips. Finally, trim the
work and mount it on a piece of folded card. One
particularly effective way of mounting is to stick the
design behind a window cut from card. The colour of the
mount should contrast strongly with that of the design.

WINDOW STENCIL

TEMPLATE

window
mount   gummed
shape   card

OVERLAPPING DESIGN

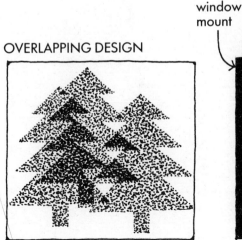

Cracker cards

Age range
Seven plus.

Group size
Individuals.

What you need
Card,
scissors,
pinking shears (optional),
gummed paper shapes
or sequins.

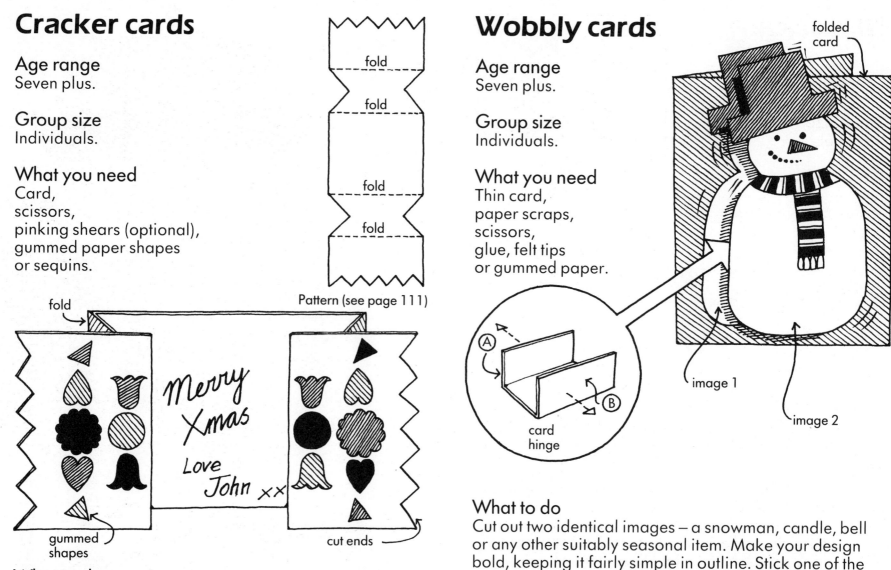

Pattern (see page 111)

What to do
Use the template outlined on page 111 to draw the cracker shape on to the card. Cut out and fold as indicated. Decorate with gummed paper shapes or sequins; use pinking shears to give decorative ends.

Wobbly cards

Age range
Seven plus.

Group size
Individuals.

What you need
Thin card,
paper scraps,
scissors,
glue, felt tips
or gummed paper.

What to do
Cut out two identical images – a snowman, candle, bell or any other suitably seasonal item. Make your design bold, keeping it fairly simple in outline. Stick one of the images to a folded card, and decorate the second image with gummed paper or felt tips. Next, make a card hinge as shown in the diagram. Stick side A to the image stuck to the card, and side B to the second image. The result is a double-image 'wobbly' card.

3D tree card

Age range
Seven plus.

Group size
Individuals.

What you need
Thin card,
coloured paper scraps,
sequins,
scissors.

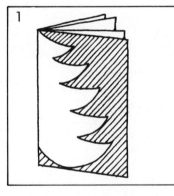

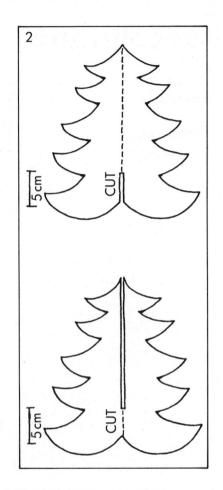

What to do
Take two rectangles of card and fold them in half. Cut out
a Christmas tree shape (1). Make sure that the base is
curved, as this helps the card to stand up well. Open both
cards out and decorate them with gummed paper shapes
or sequins. Keep clear of the fold line. When all sides are
finished, cut a slit down the fold line of the first shape to
within 5cm of the base. Cut a slit upwards from the base
of the second shape for the length of 5cm (2). Slot
together the two sections and open out the 'branches'.
Write your message above the base lines.

Santa cards

Age range
Seven plus.

Group size
Individuals.

What you need
Thin card
or stiff paper,
scissors,
paints or
felt tips.

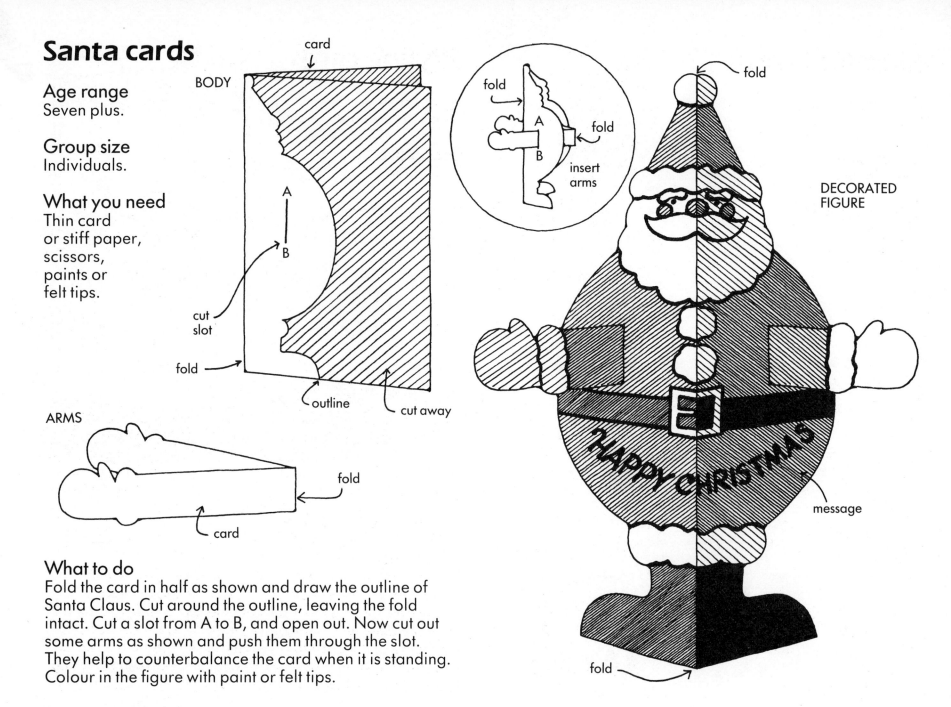

BODY

card

A
B

cut
slot

fold

outline

cut away

fold

fold

A
B

insert
arms

DECORATED
FIGURE

HAPPY CHRISTMAS

message

fold

ARMS

fold

card

What to do
Fold the card in half as shown and draw the outline of
Santa Claus. Cut around the outline, leaving the fold
intact. Cut a slot from A to B, and open out. Now cut out
some arms as shown and push them through the slot.
They help to counterbalance the card when it is standing.
Colour in the figure with paint or felt tips.

14

Multifold cards

Age range
Seven plus.

Group size
Individuals.

What you need
Stiff paper
or thin card,
felt tips or
gummed paper,
scissors.

What to do
Fold a rectangle of card or stiff paper as shown (1). Draw
on a seasonal design which will join on the fold lines (2).
Cut it out and then decorate. Write messages across the
base or on the reverse side (3).

CANDLE DESIGN

Merry Christmas

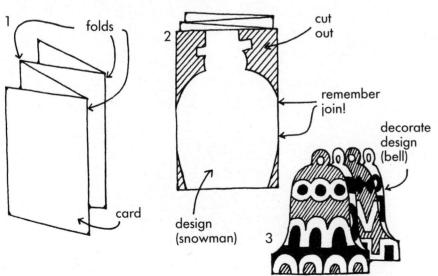

1 folds

card

2 cut out

remember join!

decorate design (bell)

design (snowman)

3

Skyline cards

Age range
Seven to eight plus.

Group size
Individuals.

What you need
White card,
strip of black or
dark-coloured paper,
fine felt tip,
white crayon or
glitter.

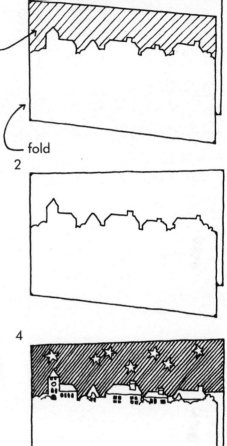

1 card

cut out

fold

2

3 glue on strip and decorate

Happy Xmas Love from Jill

4

What to do
Fold a rectangular section of card in half. Draw in the
skyline of a village (Bethlehem, say, or snowy roofs)
about one-third of the way from the top of the card, and
cut it out carefully. Stick black or dark-coloured paper on
the inside of the card to give a night sky effect. Add some
stars with a white crayon or with glitter. Add details to the
front of the card with a fine felt tip.

15

Tree decorations

A four-pointed star

Age range
Seven plus.

Group size
Individuals.

What you need
Squares of stiff paper
or thin card
(coloured one side)
ruler,
scissors, string.

PLAN

Octahedral stars

Age range
Seven plus.

Group size
Individuals.

What you need
Squares of paper
or thin card,
ruler,
scissors,
glue,
scraps of paper
or sequins.

PLAN

stick

Template on page 112

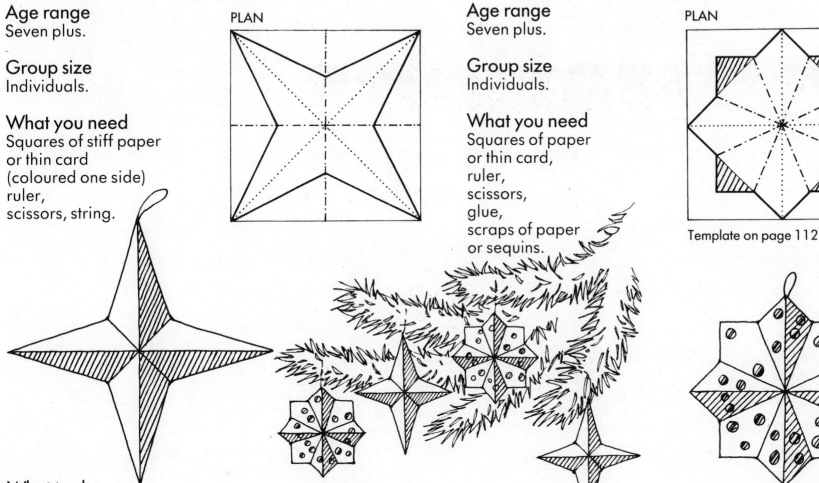

What to do
Fold the paper or card in half with the coloured side
facing. Fold in half the other way, still with the coloured
side facing. Then fold along both diagonals in turn with
the other sides facing. Mark halfway along each of the
creases made in the first two folds. Draw in the star and
cut it out. Thread some string through the top.

What to do
Cut out two eight-pointed stars from the paper or card
(see page 112). Score and fold as indicated in the
diagram. Place the two stars back to back, and stick
the shaded triangles together. Decorate with coloured
paper or sequins.

17

Peep-in octagonal star

Age range
Seven plus.

Group size
Individuals.

What you need
Squares of coloured
paper,
ruler,
scissors,
glue,
sequins or
scraps of paper.

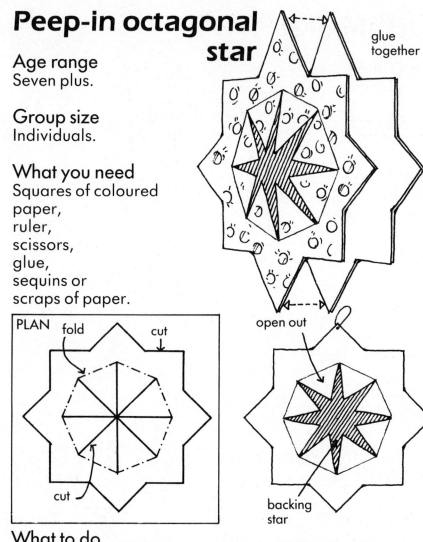

What to do
Cut, score and fold two octagonal stars as shown in the diagram on page 17. Cut slits in the centre as shown. Next, cut out two more stars from paper. Glue a star with slits on top of a plain one, allowing the one underneath to show through when the triangular flaps are lifted up. Repeat and mount both the double stars back to back.

Peep-in hexagonal star

Age range
Seven plus.

Group size
Individuals.

What you need
Black paper or card,
squares of coloured
paper, ruler,
scissors,
glue,
sequins or
coloured paper scraps.

Template on page 112

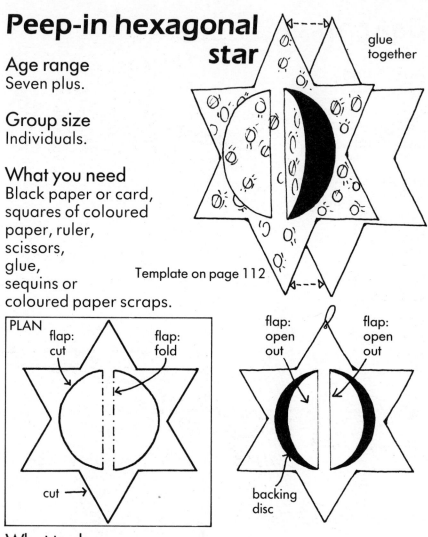

What to do
Cut a disc from black card with a radius of about 6 cm; if black paper is used, cut two discs and stick them back to back for strength. From the squares of paper draw and cut two hexagonal stars (see page 112). Score and fold as shown in the diagram. Lifting up the two semi-circular flaps, glue the stars on either side of the disc.

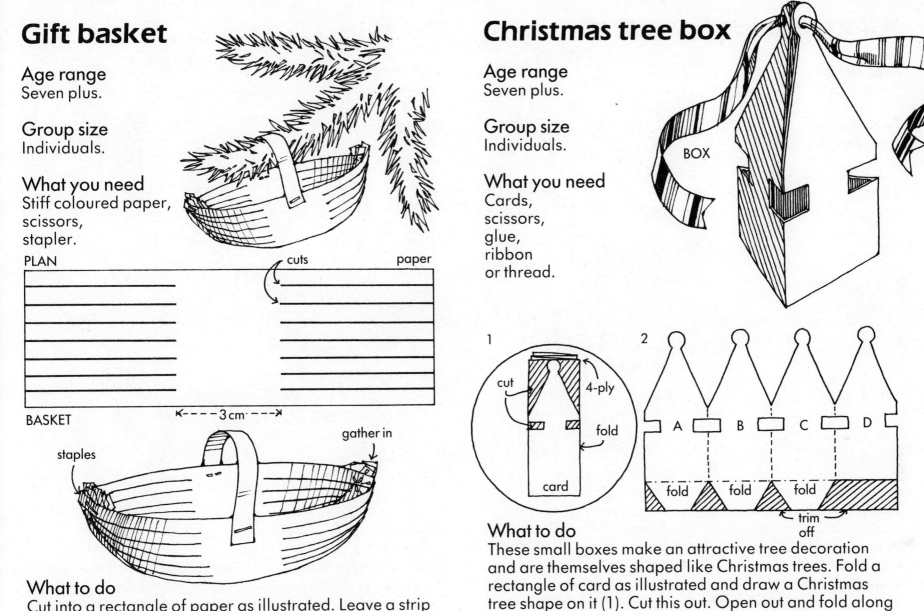

Gift basket

Age range
Seven plus.

Group size
Individuals.

What you need
Stiff coloured paper,
scissors,
stapler.

PLAN

cuts   paper

BASKET |←---- 3 cm ----→|

staples   gather in

What to do
Cut into a rectangle of paper as illustrated. Leave a strip of about 3 cm between the cut edges. Gather together the strips and staple together. Finally, fix on a further paper strip to make a handle.

Christmas tree box

Age range
Seven plus.

Group size
Individuals.

What you need
Cards,
scissors,
glue,
ribbon
or thread.

BOX

1

cut   4-ply

fold

card

2

A   B   C   D

fold   fold   fold   trim off

What to do
These small boxes make an attractive tree decoration and are themselves shaped like Christmas trees. Fold a rectangle of card as illustrated and draw a Christmas tree shape on it (1). Cut this out. Open out and fold along base to form the bottom of the box. Trim as shown (2). Stick side D to side A. Fold the base underneath, and stick. Thread a ribbon or thread through the top.

All square for Christmas

Age range
Nine plus.

Group size
Individuals.

What you need
Stiff card,
ruler,
scissors,
glue,
ribbon,
felt tips or glitter.

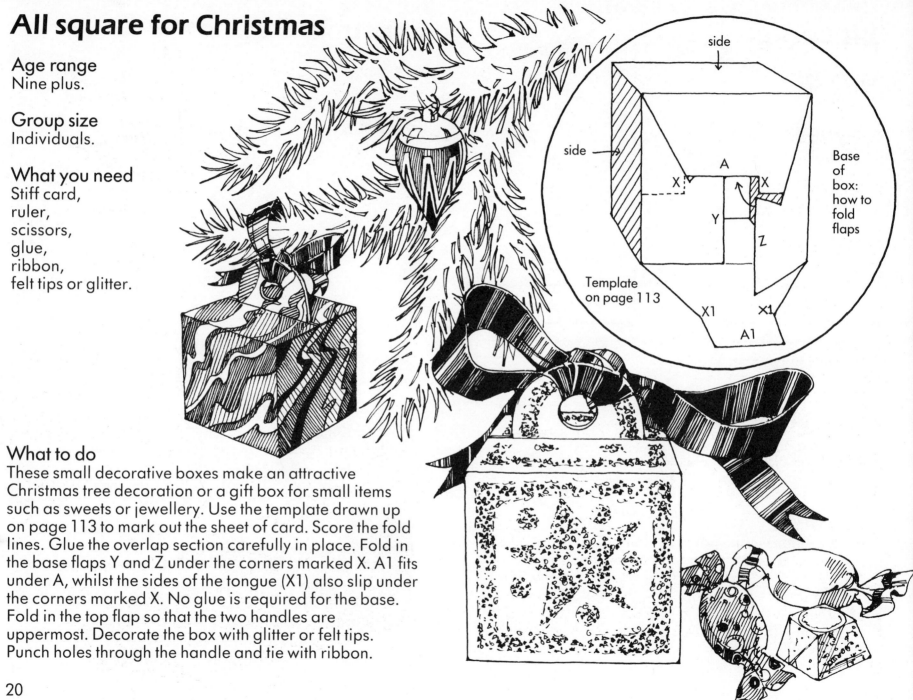

Base
of
box:
how to
fold
flaps

Template
on page 113

What to do
These small decorative boxes make an attractive
Christmas tree decoration or a gift box for small items
such as sweets or jewellery. Use the template drawn up
on page 113 to mark out the sheet of card. Score the fold
lines. Glue the overlap section carefully in place. Fold in
the base flaps Y and Z under the corners marked X. A1 fits
under A, whilst the sides of the tongue (X1) also slip under
the corners marked X. No glue is required for the base.
Fold in the top flap so that the two handles are
uppermost. Decorate the box with glitter or felt tips.
Punch holes through the handle and tie with ribbon.

20

Tree shoes

Age range
Nine plus.

Group size
Individuals.

What you need
Needle and thread,
scissors,
felt, scraps for decoration
such as beads,
fur, lace,
wool, etc.

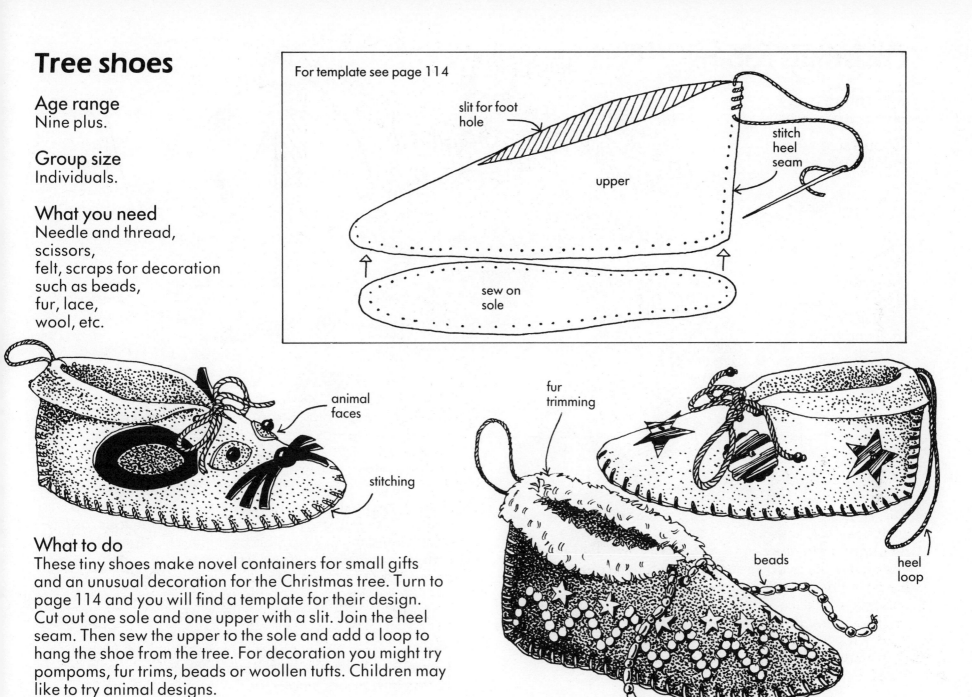

For template see page 114

slit for foot hole

stitch heel seam

upper

sew on sole

animal faces

stitching

fur trimming

beads

heel loop

What to do
These tiny shoes make novel containers for small gifts and an unusual decoration for the Christmas tree. Turn to page 114 and you will find a template for their design. Cut out one sole and one upper with a slit. Join the heel seam. Then sew the upper to the sole and add a loop to hang the shoe from the tree. For decoration you might try pompoms, fur trims, beads or woollen tufts. Children may like to try animal designs.

Christmas robins

Age range
Seven plus.

Group size
Individuals.

What you need
Scissors,
paper,
thread,
felt scraps,
feather (optional),
and *either*
card and glue
or card,
felt,
needle.

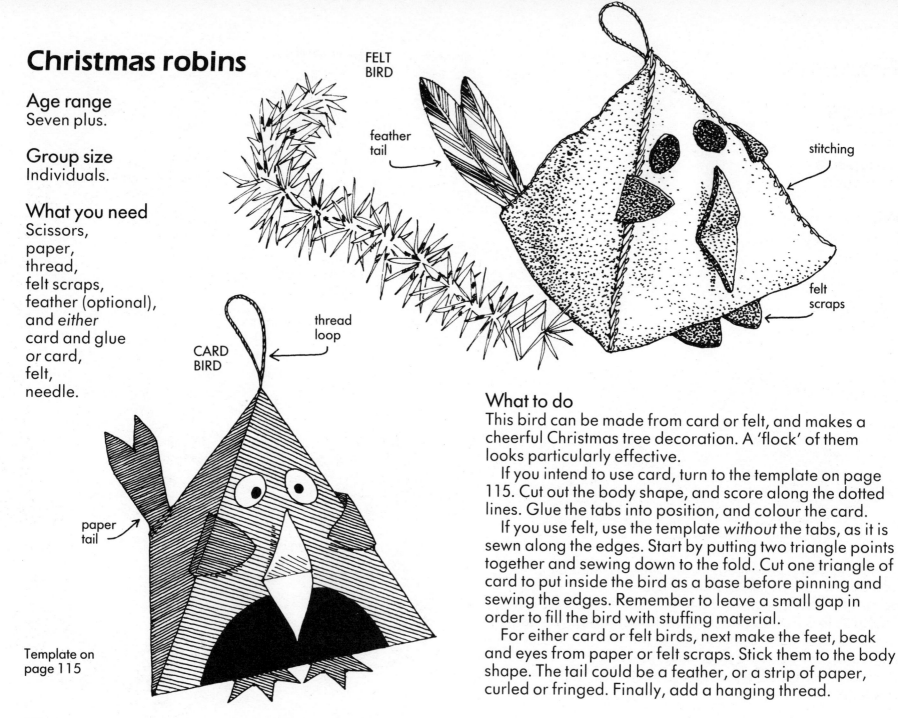

FELT
BIRD

feather
tail

stitching

felt
scraps

CARD
BIRD

thread
loop

paper
tail

Template on
page 115

What to do
This bird can be made from card or felt, and makes a
cheerful Christmas tree decoration. A 'flock' of them
looks particularly effective.

If you intend to use card, turn to the template on page
115. Cut out the body shape, and score along the dotted
lines. Glue the tabs into position, and colour the card.

If you use felt, use the template *without* the tabs, as it is
sewn along the edges. Start by putting two triangle points
together and sewing down to the fold. Cut one triangle of
card to put inside the bird as a base before pinning and
sewing the edges. Remember to leave a small gap in
order to fill the bird with stuffing material.

For either card or felt birds, next make the feet, beak
and eyes from paper or felt scraps. Stick them to the body
shape. The tail could be a feather, or a strip of paper,
curled or fringed. Finally, add a hanging thread.

Angels

Age range
Seven plus.

Group size
Individuals.

What you need
Stiff paper or
thin card,
adhesive,
and decorations
such as glitter,
sequins,
tinsel
or gummed paper.

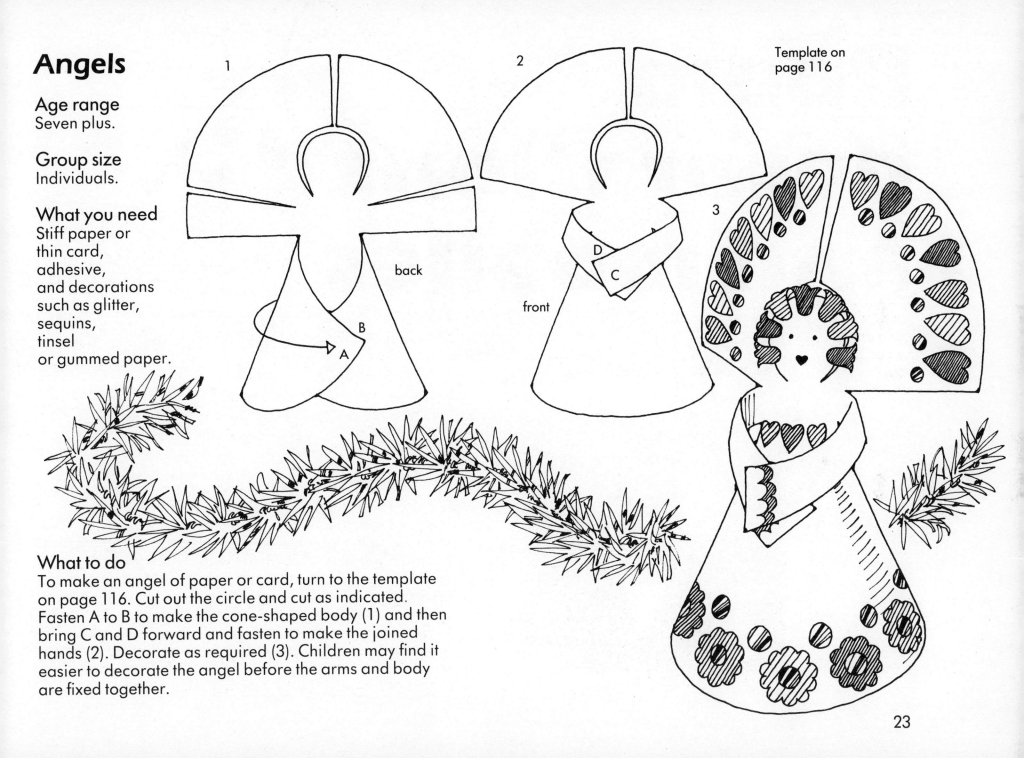

Template on
page 116

1

back

2

front

3

D

C

B

A

What to do
To make an angel of paper or card, turn to the template
on page 116. Cut out the circle and cut as indicated.
Fasten A to B to make the cone-shaped body (1) and then
bring C and D forward and fasten to make the joined
hands (2). Decorate as required (3). Children may find it
easier to decorate the angel before the arms and body
are fixed together.

Room decorations and mobiles

Simple festoons

Age range
Five plus.

Group size
Individuals.

What you need
Coloured card
or old Christmas
cards,
drinking straws,
scissors,
pinking shears
(optional),
string, thread
or wool.

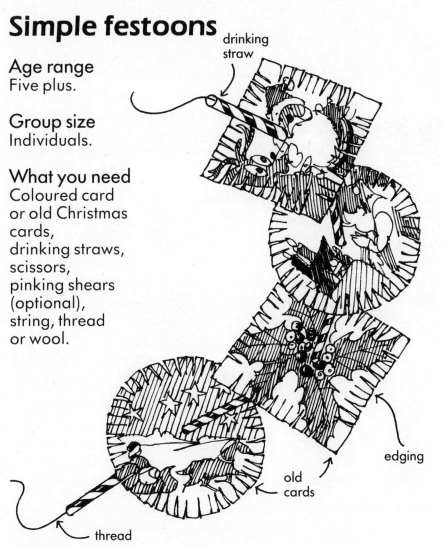

drinking
straw

edging

old
cards

thread

What to do
Find some old Christmas cards, or cut a sheet of coloured
card into squares and circles. Decorate the edges of the
cards with pinking shears or scissors. Cut each drinking
straw into four equal parts. Thread these sections on to
the line, alternately with the decorated cards.

Simple garlands

Age range
Five plus.

Group size
Individuals.

What you need
Polystyrene packing shapes,
drinking straws,
needle,
strong thread,
bar of soap.

thread

polystyrene
packing
shape

drinking
straw

What to do
Cut up the drinking straws into short lengths. Thread the
polystyrene shapes alternately with sections of drinking
straw until a suitable length of garland has been made.
For ease of threading through the polystyrene shapes,
regularly plunge the threading needle into the soap.

Ladder streamers

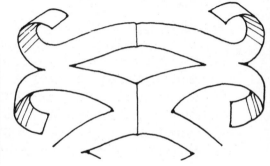

Age range
Five plus.

Group size
Individuals or pairs.

What you need
10 squares of paper,
glue,
scissors,
ruler,
sticky tape or
stapler.

What to do
To make a wide ladder streamer, lay two squares of paper on top of one another, with the 'wrong' sides facing. Glue them together along the vertical edges to a width of about 5 mm. Fold the paper in half vertically, and cut as shown. Open out carefully and join two shapes together at A. Pull gently to make the 'ladder'.

For a narrow ladder streamer, fold one square in half and glue along the vertical edge, again, to a width of about 5 mm. Fold in half again and cut as shown in the diagram. Open out and secure at B. Pull out.

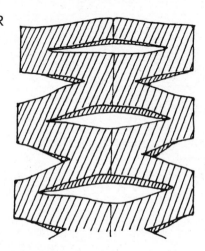

NARROW STREAMER

glue edge (5 mm in)

cut

fold

B

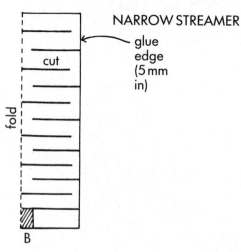

For a 'curly' ladder, fold a square in half and cut strips as shown in the diagram. Open out carefully. Curl the end strips upwards and downwards. Stretch the ladder.

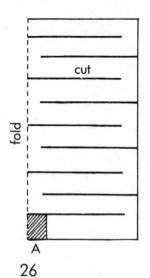

WIDE STREAMER

cut

fold

A

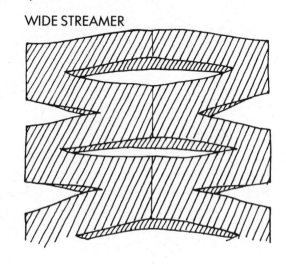

CURLY STREAMER

fold

cut

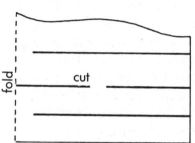

Paper bells and balls

Age range
Five plus.

Group size
Individuals.

What you need
8 squares of paper,
glue,
card for template,
scissors.

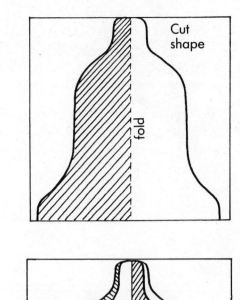

Cut shape

fold

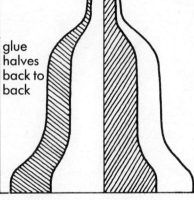

glue
halves
back to
back

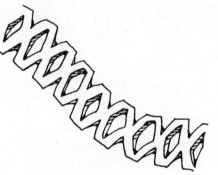

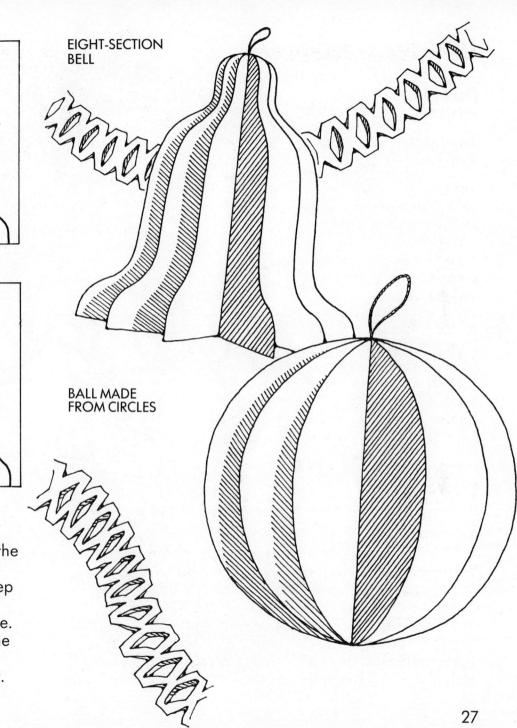

EIGHT-SECTION BELL

BALL MADE FROM CIRCLES

What to do
Use eight squares of paper. Fold each one in half with the 'wrong' sides outwards. Use a template to cut all the shapes exactly the same size, taking care always to keep the fold edge of the template to the fold of the paper. Glue the halves back to back until the shape is complete.

A bell is a good shape to try; other examples using the same principle might include balls, pear drops or hexagonal stars. Six parts may be used instead of eight.

Reindeer faces

Age range
Five plus.

Group size
Individuals or small groups.

What you need
Large sheets of paper,
brown paper,
gummed paper (for features),
twigs or
black paper.

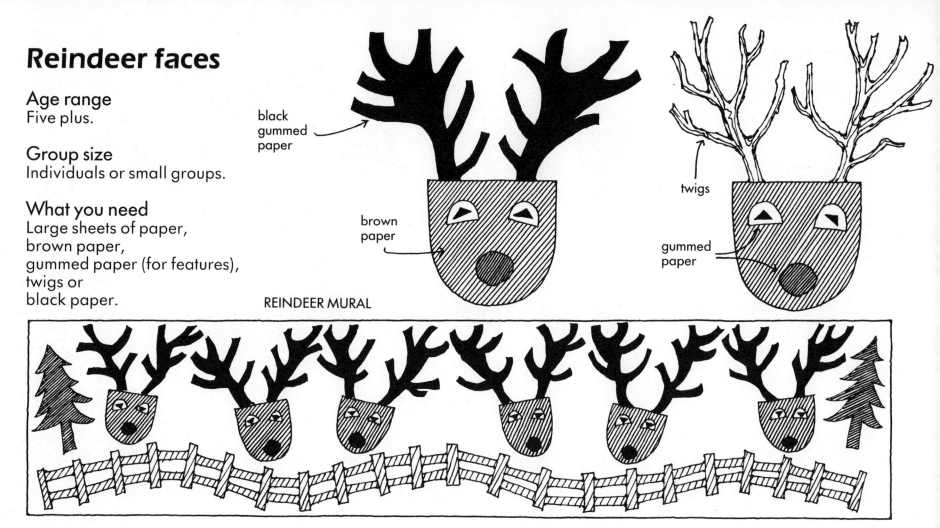

REINDEER MURAL

What to do
Cut out U-shapes from the brown paper and fix to a backing sheet on the wall. Cut features out of gummed paper, and add antlers. These too can be of gummed paper, or of twigs and branches. Group the heads together to make a pleasing pattern. The children might like to add a picket fence along the bottom.

For a 3D effect the children can 'pleat' the face, fixing it at the nose with gummed paper.

3D REINDEER

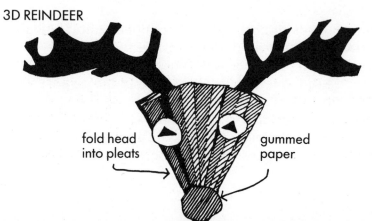

28

Paper chains

Age range
Six plus.

Group size
Small or large groups.

What you need
Paper,
scissors.

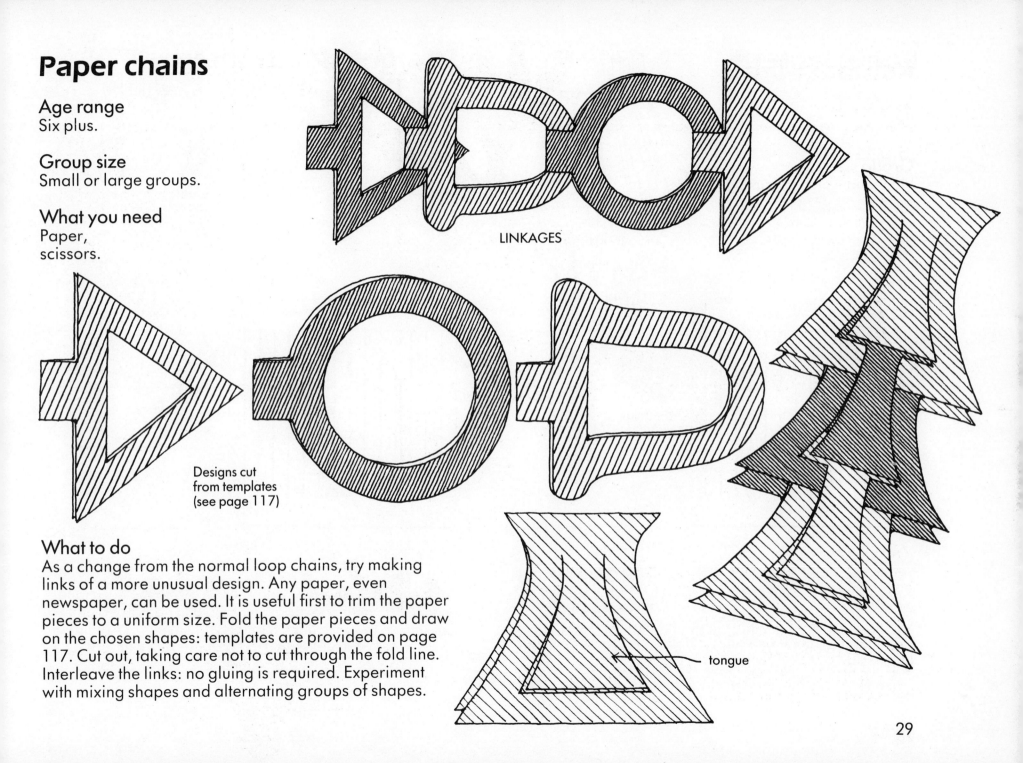

LINKAGES

Designs cut
from templates
(see page 117)

tongue

What to do
As a change from the normal loop chains, try making
links of a more unusual design. Any paper, even
newspaper, can be used. It is useful first to trim the paper
pieces to a uniform size. Fold the paper pieces and draw
on the chosen shapes: templates are provided on page
117. Cut out, taking care not to cut through the fold line.
Interleave the links: no gluing is required. Experiment
with mixing shapes and alternating groups of shapes.

Barrel lantern

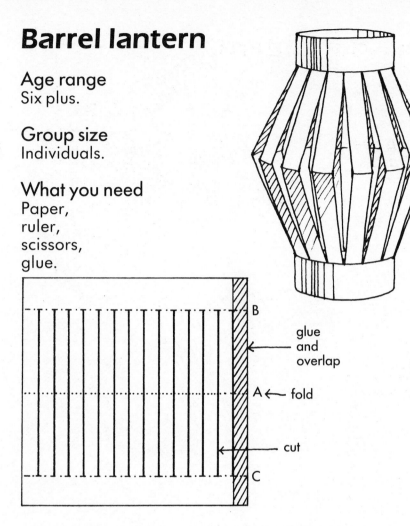

Age range
Six plus.

Group size
Individuals.

What you need
Paper,
ruler,
scissors,
glue.

B

glue
and
overlap

A ← fold

cut

C

What to do
There are many different ways of making Christmas lanterns. This is the traditional design. Take a square of paper. Score it along the horizontal design as shown in the diagram. Fold it in half along line A. Cut slits up to the score lines B and C, at 1 cm intervals. Now flatten out the fold. To make a cylinder, glue the last strip on top of the first one. Allow the vertical strips to 'barrel' out.

Straight-sided lantern

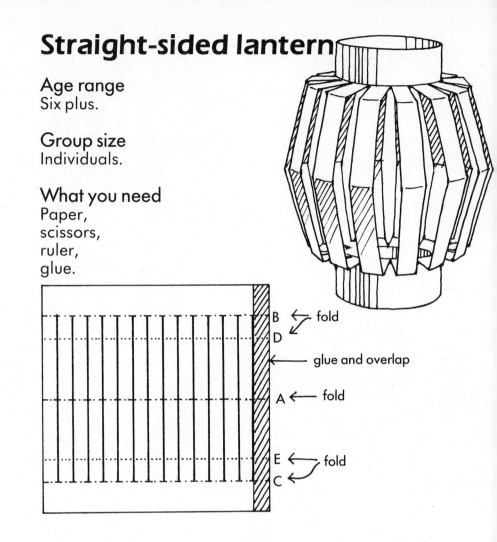

Age range
Six plus.

Group size
Individuals.

What you need
Paper,
scissors,
ruler,
glue.

B ← fold
D

glue and overlap

A ← fold

E ← fold
C

What to do
Take a square of paper and score it along the horizontal lines as shown in the diagram. Fold it in half along line A. Cut slits up to score lines B and C at 1 cm intervals. Flatten out this fold and make new folds along score lines B, D, E and C. To make a cylinder, glue the last strip on top of the first one.

Waisted lantern

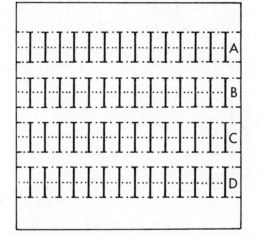

Age range
Six plus.

Group size
Individuals.

What you need
Paper,
scissors,
ruler,
glue.

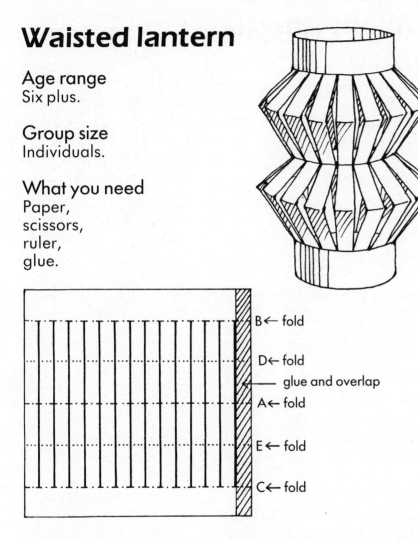

B ← fold
D ← fold
— glue and overlap
A ← fold
E ← fold
C ← fold

What to do
Take a square of paper and score it along the horizontal lines as shown in the diagram. Fold it in half along line A. Cut slits up to score lines B and C at 1 cm intervals. Flatten out the fold, and then make folds along score lines B, C, D and E. To make a cylinder glue the last strip on top of the first one.

Four-bar lantern

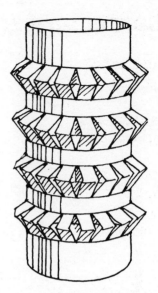

Age range
Six plus.

Group size
Individuals.

What you need
Paper,
scissors,
rulers,
sticky tape.

A
B
C
D

What to do
Take a square of paper and score it along the dotted lines shown. On the back, at right angles to the scoring, draw lines at 1 cm intervals. Fold, with the right sides facing along line A, and cut 1 cm slits up to the next line of scoring. Reverse the fold. Repeat with folds B, C and D. Score and fold the other eight lines with the right sides facing. Make a cylinder by fastening the back on the inside.

Inside-out lantern

Age range
Six plus.

Group size
Individuals.

What you need
Paper,
ruler,
scissors,
glue.

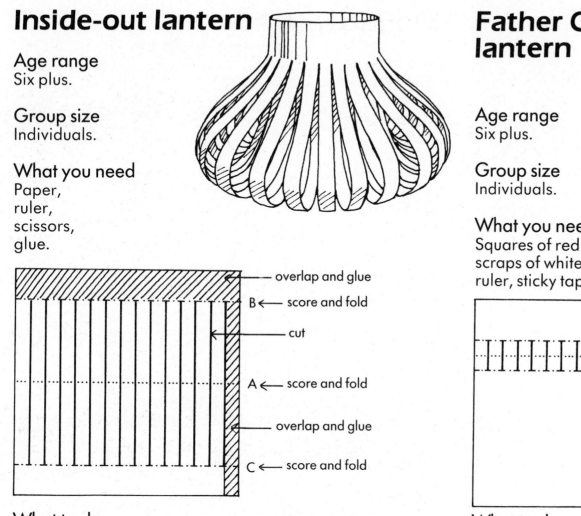

- overlap and glue
- B ← score and fold
- cut
- A ← score and fold
- overlap and glue
- C ← score and fold

What to do
Take a square of paper and score it along the horizontal lines as shown in the diagram. Fold it in half along line A, and then cut up to the score lines B and C at 1 cm intervals. Flatten out the central fold and then fold along the other two scored lines. Overlap and glue the top and bottom uncut sections together, and then overlap and glue the end strips to make a cylinder.

Father Christmas lantern

Age range
Six plus.

Group size
Individuals.

What you need
Squares of red card or paper, scraps of white paper, scissors, ruler, sticky tape, glue.

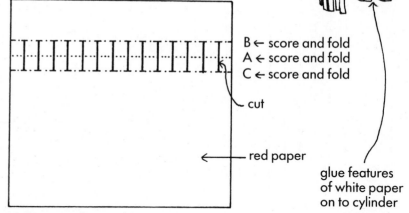

- B ← score and fold
- A ← score and fold
- C ← score and fold
- cut
- red paper
- glue features of white paper on to cylinder

What to do
Score and fold a square of red paper or card along line A, the 'wrong' sides facing. Cut 1 cm slits as indicated by the thick black lines in the diagram. Score and fold lines B and C with the 'right' sides facing. Make a cylinder by fastening the back with sticky tape on the inside. Cut the features from white paper and curl the moustache and beard. Stick them on to the front of the cylinder.

Lace 'lampshades'

Age range
Six plus.

Group size
Individuals or small groups.

What you need
Round balloon,
tissue paper,
scissors.

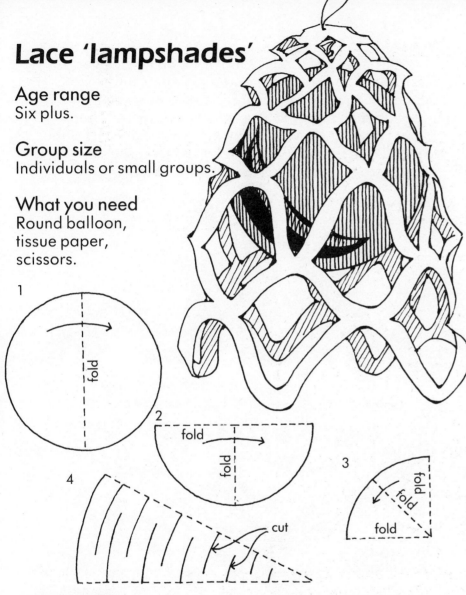

1

fold

2

fold
fold

3

fold
fold
fold

4

cut

What to do
Cut out a circle of tissue paper (1) and fold as shown in
stages (2) and (3). Cut carefully as indicated in stage (4)
and open out the cuts by pulling gently. Place the net over
a round balloon and hang it up.

Stringamabobs

Age range
Six plus.

Group size
Pairs.

What you need
Balloons,
string,
PVA adhesive.

string

PVA
adhesive

balloon

What to do
Blow up a balloon. Tie and hold the neck and thoroughly
coat the surface of the balloon with PVA adhesive.
Gradually bind the balloon with string. Keep on applying
the PVA as you wind the string, until a reasonable
covering is achieved. When the PVA adhesive has dried,
the balloon can be popped! Hang up the balls.

Christmas sweet hangings

Age range
Seven plus.

Group size
Small groups.

What you need
Wire coat hangers, green crêpe paper, scissors, tinsel, ribbons, sweets, thread.

What to do
This attractive hanging is ideal for a children's party. First, bend the wire coat hangers to make the basic frame, fixing the ends securely. Cover the wire frame with fringed crêpe paper to give a lush, evergreen effect. Make two large bows from tinsel and/or ribbon for the top and base. Finally hang wrapped sweets at varying heights from the frame.

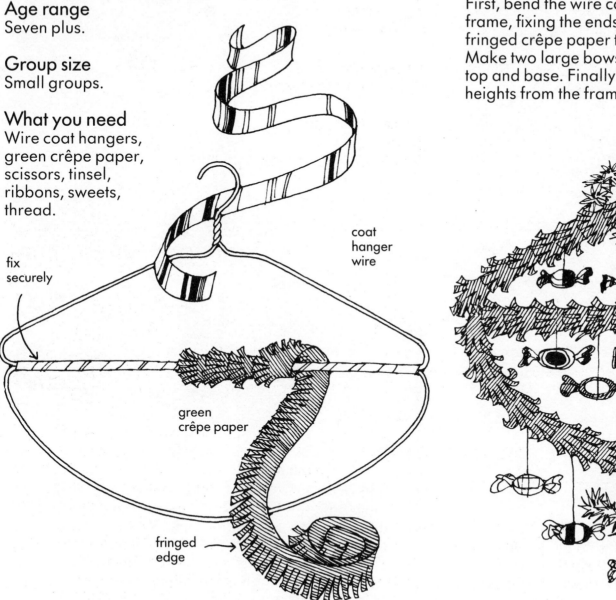

fix securely

coat hanger wire

green crêpe paper

fringed edge

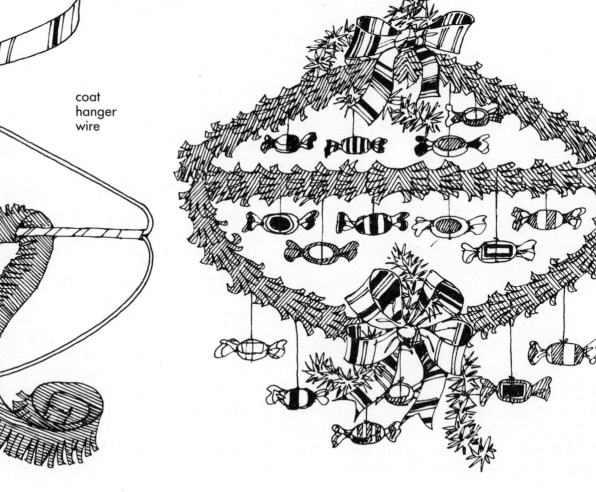

A mobile tree

Age range
Seven plus.

Group size
Individuals.

What you need
Thin card,
scissors,
felt tips or
glitter for
decoration,
thread.

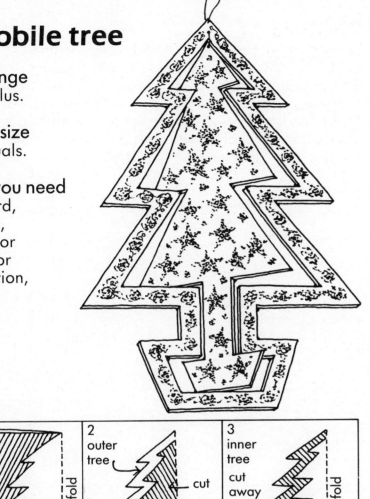

What to do
This festive mobile is made from card. Fold the card as shown and cut out the shape of a tree and pot. Cut again, as shown in (2). Finally, cut away the edges of the remaining card (3). Open out the two remaining trees. Hang the smaller tree from the larger with thread.

A mobile Santa

Age range
Seven plus.

Group size
Individuals or small groups.

What you need
Card (red, white
and black),
strong thread,
scissors,
glue.

What to do
Cut out from the red card: a large circle for the body, a triangle for the hat, a small circle for the nose. From the white card, cut out five small circles for the eyes, buttons and pompom; a moustache, and lengths of 'fur' trim. From the black card, cut out mittens, boots, a buckle, and eye spots.

Stick the pompom and trim to the hat. Stick the black spots on the eyes. Stick the nose to the moustache. Stick all the other items to the large red circle as indicated. When dry, assemble the mobile as shown.

Streamers from circles

Age range
Seven plus.

Group size
Individuals or
small groups.

What you need
10 squares of paper,
pencil,
pair of compasses,
scissors,
glue or staples,
pinking shears
(optional).

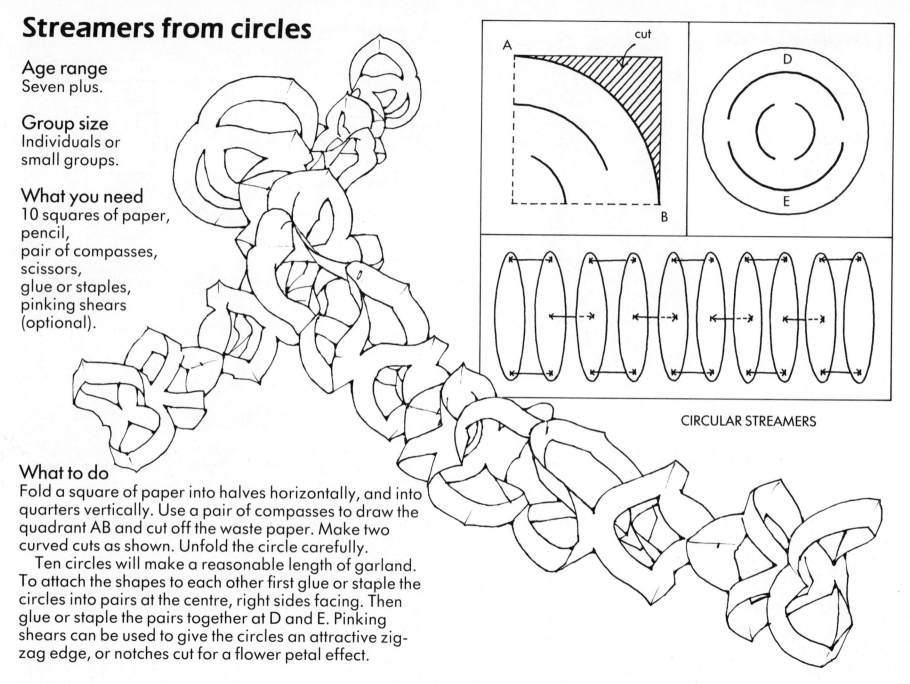

CIRCULAR STREAMERS

What to do
Fold a square of paper into halves horizontally, and into
quarters vertically. Use a pair of compasses to draw the
quadrant AB and cut off the waste paper. Make two
curved cuts as shown. Unfold the circle carefully.
   Ten circles will make a reasonable length of garland.
To attach the shapes to each other first glue or staple the
circles into pairs at the centre, right sides facing. Then
glue or staple the pairs together at D and E. Pinking
shears can be used to give the circles an attractive zig-
zag edge, or notches cut for a flower petal effect.

36

Streamers from squares

Age range
Seven plus.

Group size
Individuals or
small groups.

What you need
10 squares of paper,
glue
or long-armed stapler,
pencil,
ruler,
scissors.

SQUARE
STREAMERS

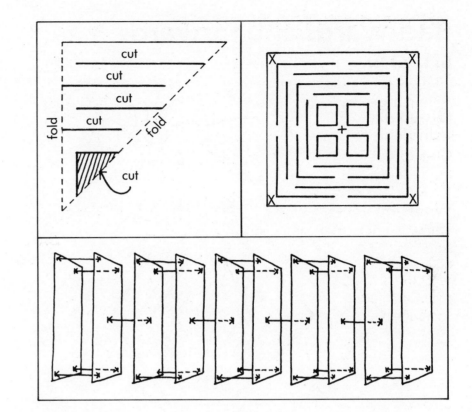

What to do

Fold a square into halves horizontally, and into quarters
vertically. Then fold into eighths along the diagonal.
Have the open edge at the top and cut four parallel slits
as shown in the diagram. Cut out the waste triangle at the
bottom, and open out the square carefully.

Mount the squares together in pairs with the 'right'
sides facing, and staple or glue at the centre. Then, using
these pairs of squares staple or glue two sets together at
the corners, ensuring that only two 'wrong' sides are
being fixed together each time.

NB All centres must be fixed before the corners
are started.

Backwards and forwards shapes

Age range
Nine plus.

Group size
Individuals.

What you need
Thin card or paper,
scissors,
thread.

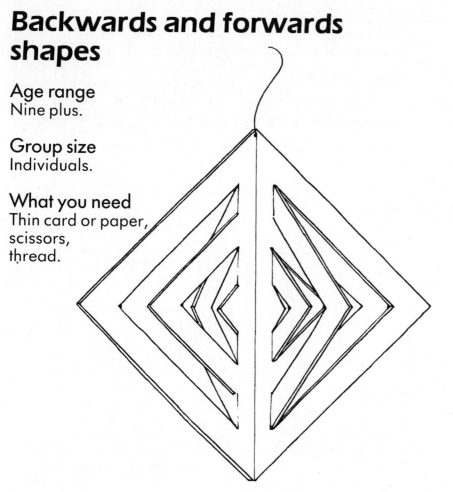

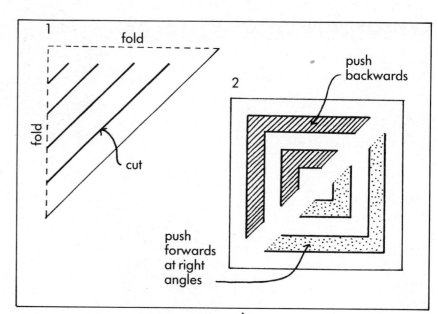

What to do
To make the square decoration, glue two paper squares
back to back, or, if using card, cut out one square only.
Fold the square into four along its diagonals, and cut slits
as shown in the diagram (1). Open out carefully.
Referring to (2), push the hatched areas backwards and
the spotted areas forwards at right angles. Hang up from
one of the points.
   A circular decoration may be made in the same way.

Umbrella mobile

Age range
Nine plus.

Group size
Small or large groups.

What you need
Old umbrella frame,
silver spray,
tinsel,
decorative items
such as card,
felt scraps,
braid ribbon,
small empty boxes,
paper.

What to do
Spray the umbrella frame with silver paint. When it has dried, wrap tinsel around the struts, taking some strands from the edge to below the handle, creating a 'maypole' effect. Hang the frame with decorations such as small parcels, stockings, Father Christmas figures, angels and stars, snowmen and snowflakes, lanterns and candles.

Patchwork trees

Age range
Five plus.

Group size
Small or large groups.

What you need
Old Christmas cards,
coloured card,
large sheets of paper,
glue,
scissors,
ruler.

What to do
Look out a selection of old Christmas cards. Cut them into triangles about 12×12×10cm. Assemble them in the shape of a tree on a sheet of backing paper, and glue them on. Add a trunk, pot and star to finish. Display the patchwork trees on the wall. Alternatively, the blank side of the Christmas cards may be used. They can be decorated with a suitable Christmas motif and displayed in the same way.

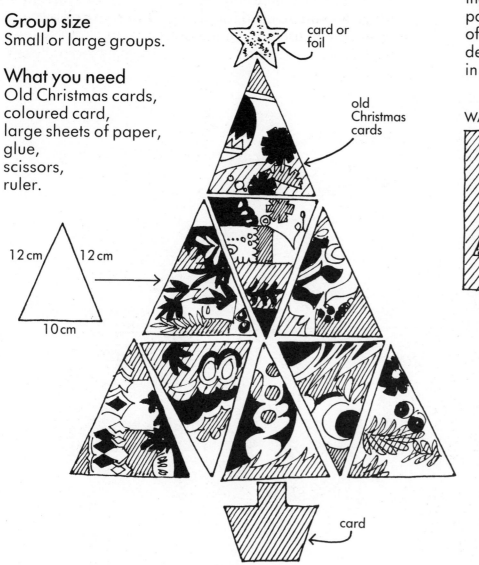

12 cm   12 cm

10 cm

card or foil

old Christmas cards

card

WALL DISPLAY

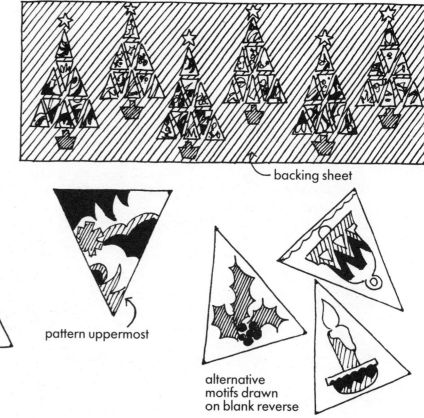

backing sheet

pattern uppermost

alternative motifs drawn on blank reverse

Balloon personalities

Age range
Seven plus.

Group size
Individuals.

What you need
Balloons,
scissors,
string,
decorative scraps of
paper, card,
felt, wool,
braids, fur,
fabric etc,
rubber solution.

What to do
Great fun can be had decorating party balloons with the faces of Christmas characters, animals, monsters etc. 'Hair' may be stuck on under conical hats or crowns. The features can be made from any suitable scraps. A rubber solution should be used for gluing. Different balloon shapes can be used. Long balloons are particularly suitable for animals and monsters. The finished balloons can be hung up in bunches.

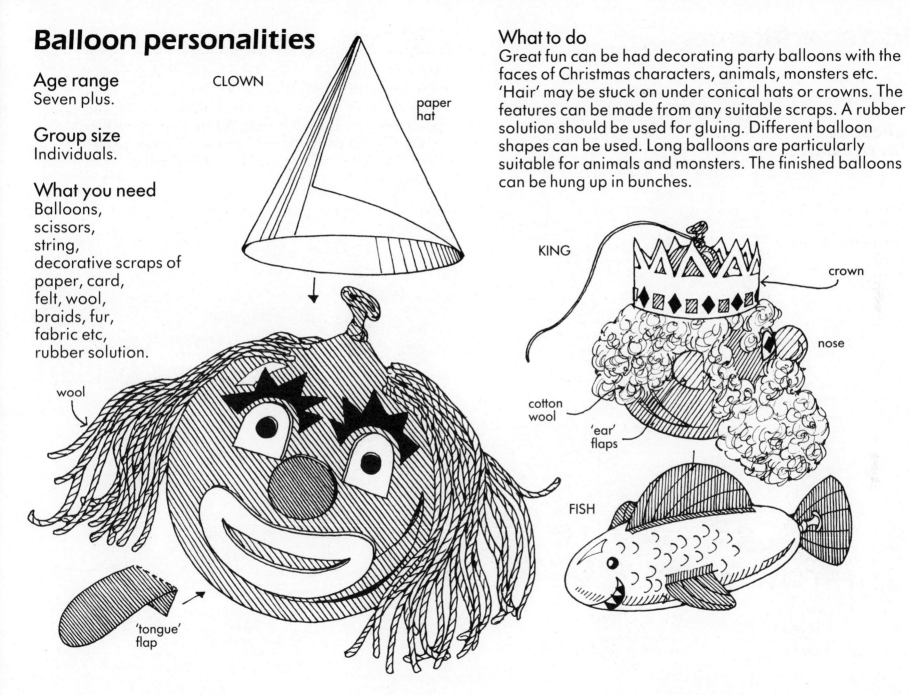

CLOWN

paper hat

wool

'tongue' flap

KING

crown

nose

cotton wool

'ear' flaps

FISH

3D Santa face

Age range
Seven plus.

Group size
Individuals or
small groups.

What you need
Scissors,
paper (white, red
and black),
glue.

What to do
This Father Christmas can be made small, large or even lifesize – the choice is yours. First, cut out the shape of the head and beard from white paper. Fringe and curl the beard (1). Now cut out a cap from red paper (2) and attach its edge to the head. Fix on a tassel of fringed and curled white paper (3). Cut the cap trimming from white paper and fringe and curl in the same way (4). Attach it to the edge of the cap. Cut the eyes and mouth from black paper (5) and glue them in position. Add a moustache of white paper and a nose of red paper. Hang on the wall or ceiling.

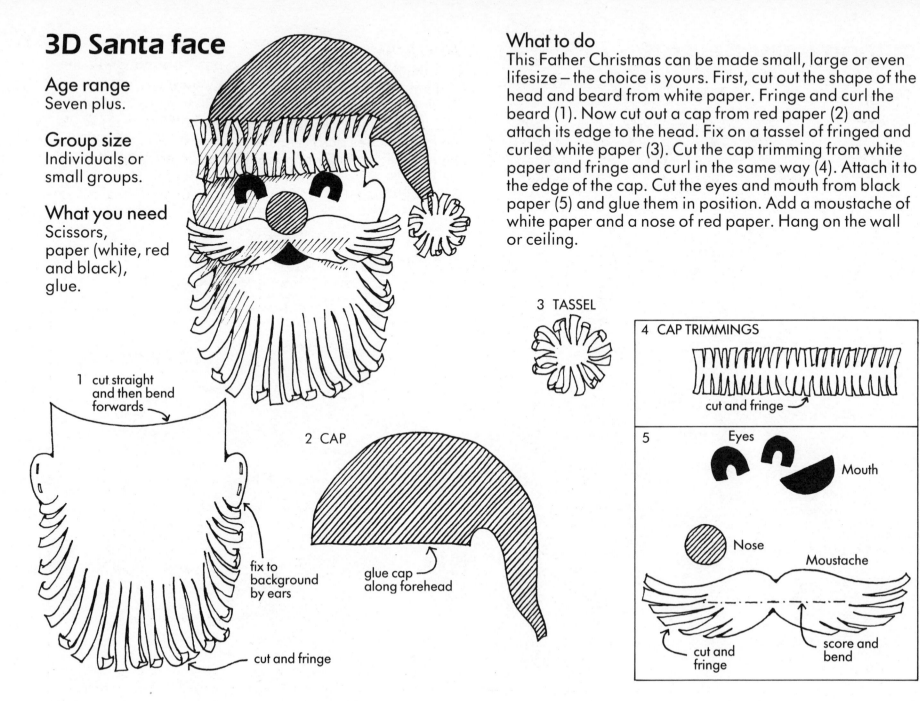

1 cut straight and then bend forwards

fix to background by ears

cut and fringe

2 CAP

glue cap along forehead

3 TASSEL

4 CAP TRIMMINGS

cut and fringe

5 Eyes

Mouth

Nose

Moustache

cut and fringe

score and bend

Snowflakes

Age range
Five plus.

Group size
Individuals.

What you need
Paper,
scissors,
glue.

What to do

This simple cutting and folding exercise can produce beautiful snowflakes for decorating windows, wall displays, or individual decorations. Take a rectangle of paper and fold it in half (1). Fold it in half again (2). Take the folded sides across to the other as shown, and trim off the remainder (3). Trim again into a curved edge (4), and cut into the sides as shown (5). Open out (6). The snowflakes can be collected and displayed as a group, stuck on a window or on a dark-coloured paper.

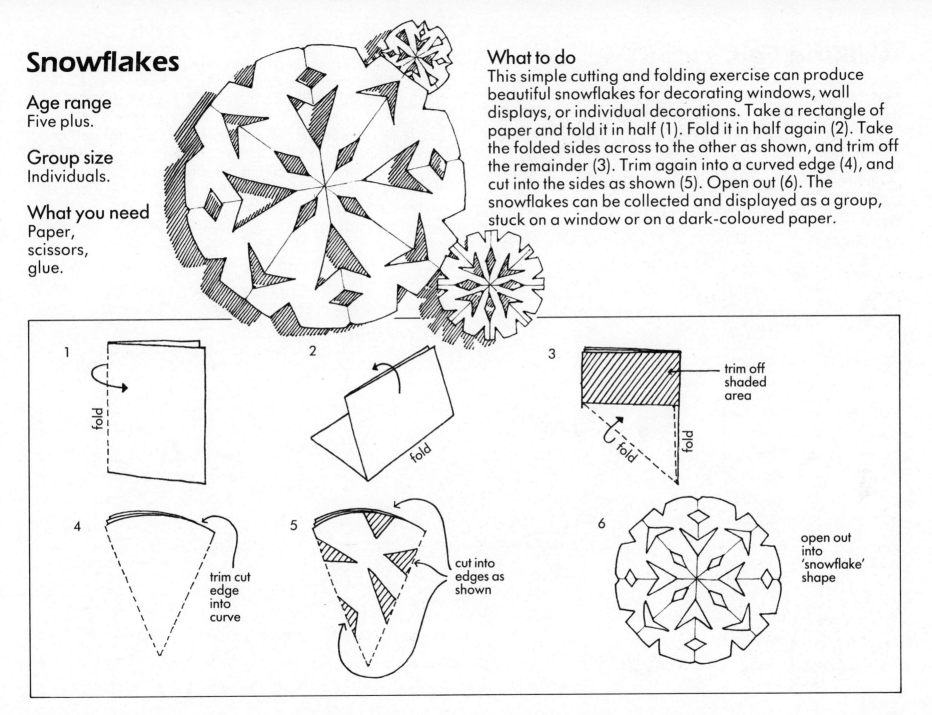

1
fold

2
fold

3
trim off shaded area
fold
fold

4
trim cut edge into curve

5
cut into edges as shown

6
open out into 'snowflake' shape

Walking figures

Age range
Seven plus.

Group size
Individuals.

What you need
Thick card,
split pin,
scissors,
crayons.

What to do
Cut out the shape of a snowman or a Santa figure from the card, and colour it in with crayons. Cut out a circle and draw on four boot shapes as shown: a template for this is provided on page 118. Attach the cut-out boots behind the figure by means of a split pin, making sure that the boots are visible. As the boots are turned, it looks as though the figure is walking. Choose any figures to make.

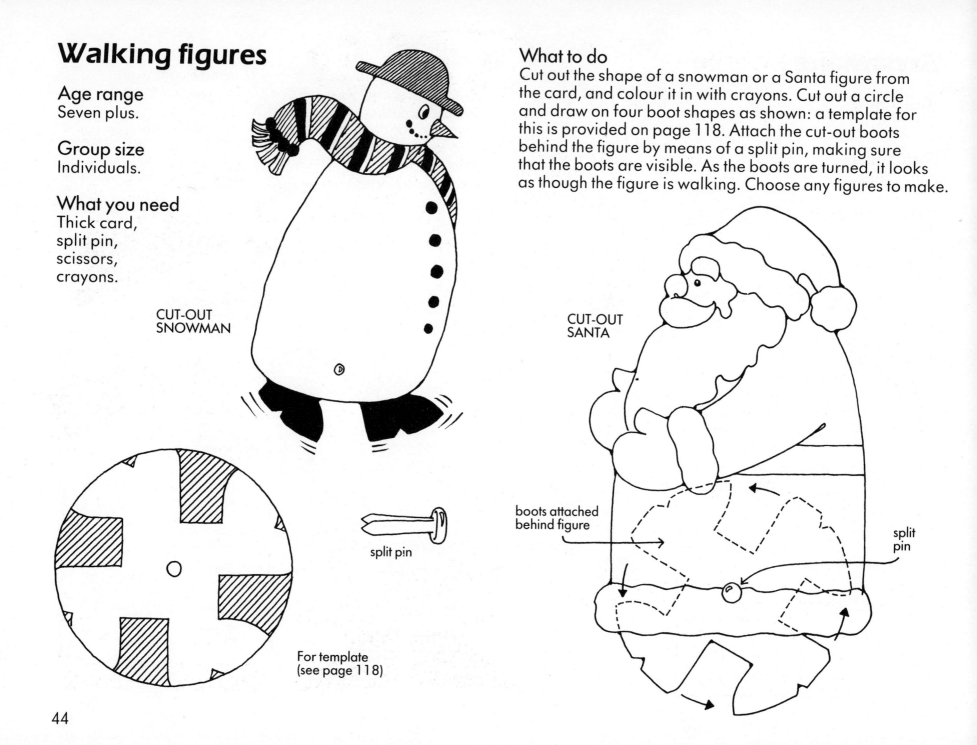

CUT-OUT
SNOWMAN

CUT-OUT
SANTA

split pin

boots attached
behind figure

split
pin

For template
(see page 118)

Expanding people

Age range
Five plus.

Group size
Individuals.

What you need
Paper,
coloured paper scraps,
glue,
scissors,
thread.

What to do
Take a rectangle of paper and fold and cut it as shown.
Open it out carefully: this forms the body. Add faces,
feet, hands etc to make Christmas characters. Experiment
with bodies of various sizes. Suspend some large models
from the ceiling, and smaller ones from the walls.

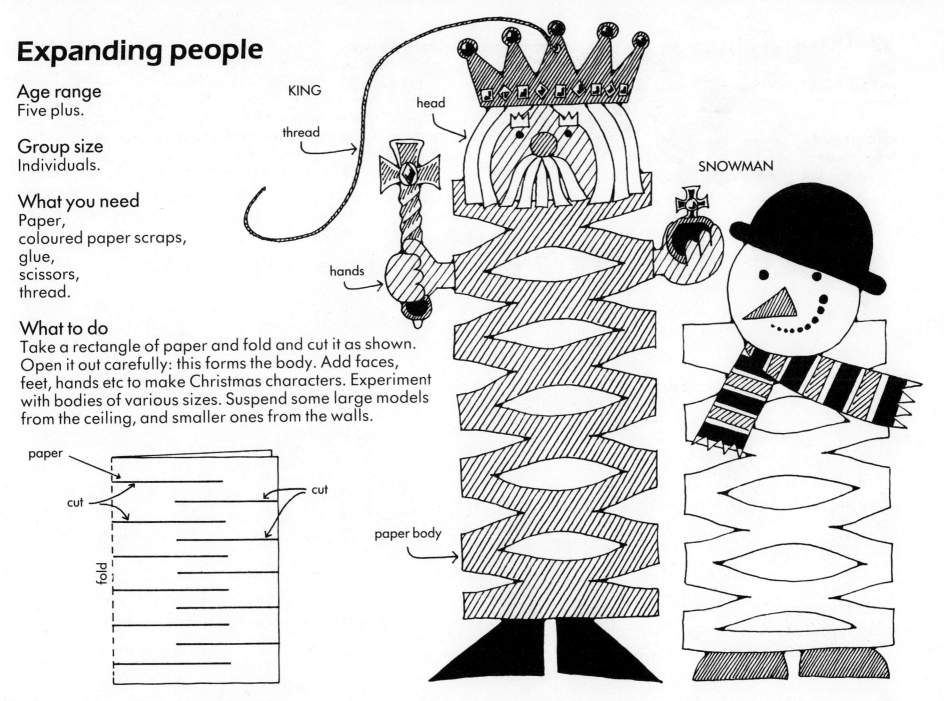

KING

thread

head

hands

paper

cut

cut

fold

paper body

SNOWMAN

Crackers and table decorations

Robin on a log

Age range
Six plus.

Group size
Individuals.

What you need
Cardboard tube,
gummed paper (brown,
red, yellow),
scissors.

What to do
This is an attractive napkin ring for the Christmas table.
Cut a cardboard tube into sections approximately 5 cm
long. Cover it with brown gummed paper, and cut a slit
as indicated (1). To make the robin, cut a body shape
from card as shown and cover in brown gummed paper
(2). Fold in half, to form the robin's back. Add a red
breast and a yellow beak (3). Cut out a wing shape as
shown (4) from brown gummed paper, slip it over the
back and stick. Wedge the body in the slit (5).

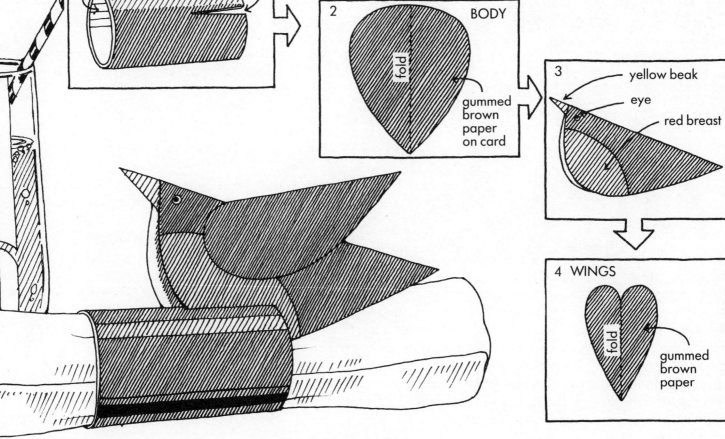

1 cardboard tube   gummed brown paper   slit

2 BODY   fold   gummed brown paper on card

3 yellow beak   eye   red breast

4 WINGS   fold   gummed brown paper

Camelot table centre

Age range
Seven plus.

Group size
Small groups.

What you need
Empty plastic containers (all shapes and sizes), metallic spray paint, cocktail sticks, black paper, card.

What to do
A Christmas castle makes an unusual table centre. Make towers from the containers, some tall, some short. Vary the heights and widths. Group them together and fix to a card base. When you are happy with the arrangement of tower shapes, spray them carefully with metallic spray paint. When this has dried, stick on black paper windows and doors. Finally add the cocktail stick flagpoles and appropriate paper flags and decorations.

Candle table centre

Age range
Seven plus.

Group size
Individuals.

What you need
Cardboard tube
paper plate,
glue,
paints,
Plasticine,
tinsel or other decorations,
ribbon,
florists wire (optional),
coloured paper.

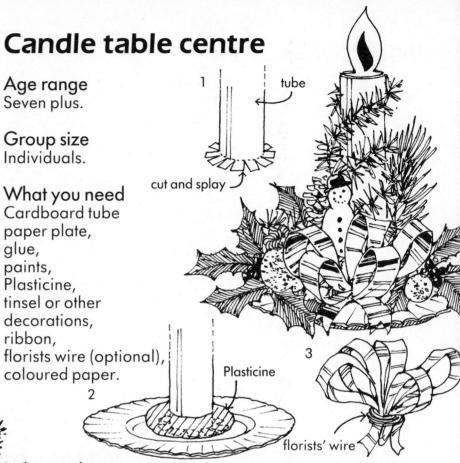

What to do
A cardboard tube makes a fine 'candle' decoration for the centre of the table. Cut one end of the tube as indicated in (1) and glue firmly on to a paper plate. When this has dried, paint the tube and drop a small amount of Plasticine down the tube in order to add some weight to the decoration. Place a roll of Plasticine around the base of the 'candle' as well (2). Add a 'flame' of coloured paper and decorate the tube with tinsel or other Christmas baubles. Push sprigs of holly firmly into the Plasticine and add some ribbon for extra finish. Use florists wire to gather ribbon in loops (3).

Birds in the bush

Age range
Seven plus.

Group size
Individuals or
small groups.

What you need
Twig,
plaster of Paris,
small container
(eg yoghurt pot),
paper (white or coloured),
tissue paper,
gummed paper,
paint (optional),
foil.

What to do
To make this table decoration you will need to fix a
branched twig into a container of plaster of Paris. If you
wish, it can then be painted white, silver or gold, but this
is optional. The container can be covered with foil.

   To make the birds, cut circles of paper and fold them in
half (1). Cut a neat slot in the sides as indicated. Pleat a
rectangle of tissue paper for the wings (2) and pass
through the slit. Open out the tissue and stick the ends
together (3). Add eyes and beaks (4), and the birds are
ready to perch on the twigs, as shown in the main picture.

   The display can look most effective if the colour is
restricted. You could try all-white birds on a white tree, or
all-red birds on a silver tree.

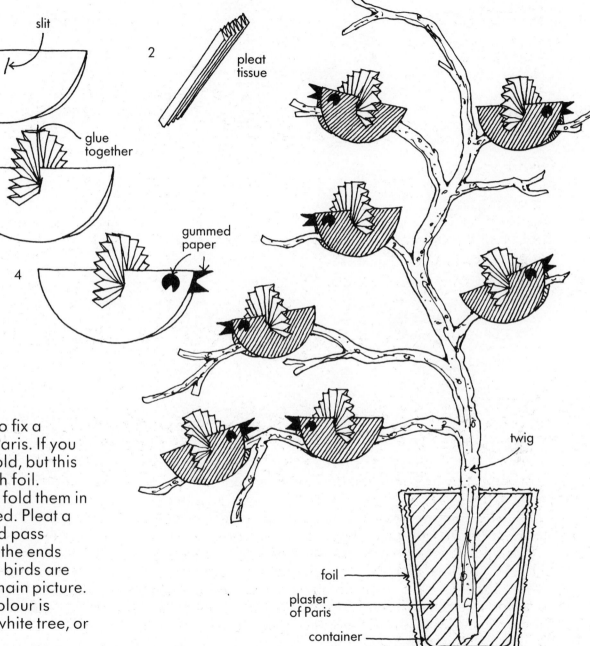

49

Minibags

Age range
Nine plus.

Group size
Individuals or small groups.

What you need
Christmas wrapping paper or other paper,
scraps of card,
ribbon or thread,
ruler,
scissors,
glue.

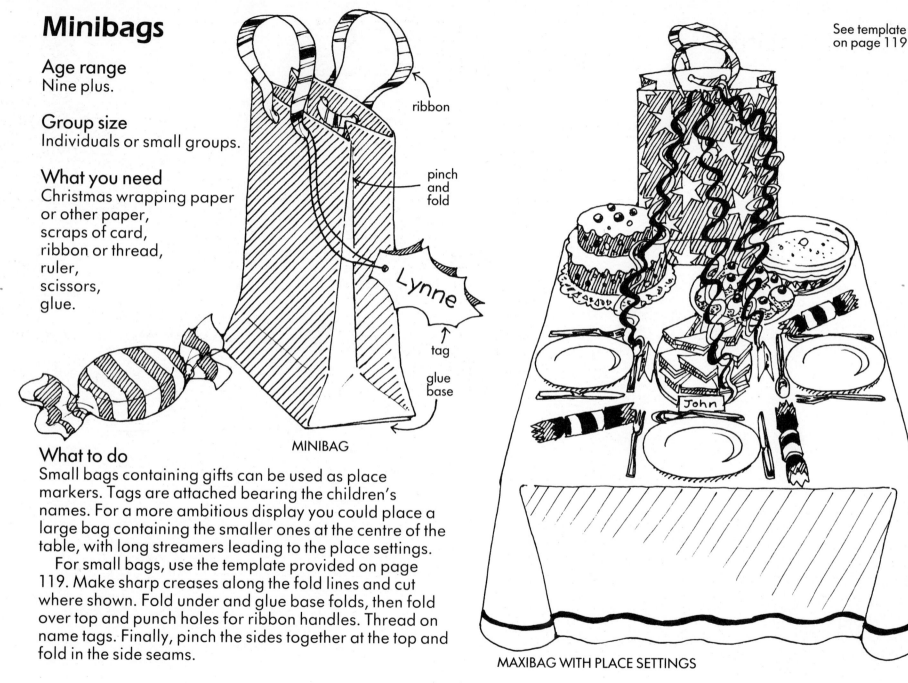

ribbon

pinch and fold

Lynne

tag

glue base

MINIBAG

See template on page 119

MAXIBAG WITH PLACE SETTINGS

John

What to do
Small bags containing gifts can be used as place markers. Tags are attached bearing the children's names. For a more ambitious display you could place a large bag containing the smaller ones at the centre of the table, with long streamers leading to the place settings.

For small bags, use the template provided on page 119. Make sharp creases along the fold lines and cut where shown. Fold under and glue base folds, then fold over top and punch holes for ribbon handles. Thread on name tags. Finally, pinch the sides together at the top and fold in the side seams.

Animal crackers

Age range
Nine plus.

Group size
Individuals.

What you need
Cardboard tubes,
tissue paper,
embroidery thread,
gummed paper,
sweets or small gifts
(optional),
scissors,
pinking shears.

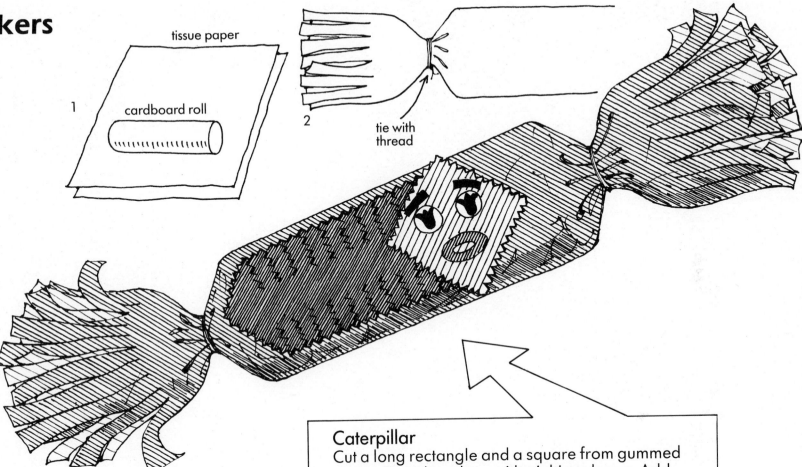

tissue paper

cardboard roll

1

2

tie with
thread

What to do
To make Christmas crackers, cut the tube to the length
required. Wrap coloured tissue paper around the tube
and glue into position (1). Two layers are best. Tie with
thread (2) around both ends (first inserting any gifts).
Fringe or curl the tissue paper ends.

You can use all kinds of motifs to decorate the cracker.
Gummed paper is ideal, and can be cut into holly leaves,
Christmas trees etc. On the following pages you will find
all kinds of examples.

Caterpillar
Cut a long rectangle and a square from gummed
paper. Trim the edges with pinking shears. Add
facial features and stick to the cracker.

rectangle

square

pinking

stick on
features

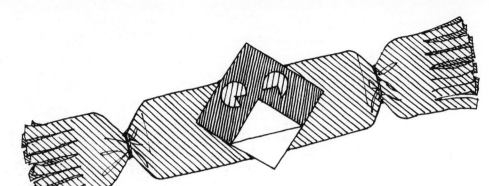

Bird

Fold a square of gummed paper in half (1) and in half again (2). Turn up a corner (one layer only) to form a beak (3). Add the eyes and stick on.

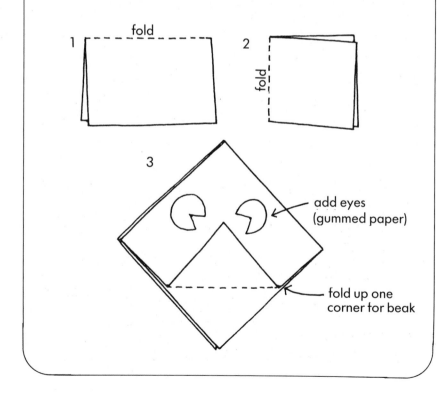

1

fold

2

fold

3

add eyes
(gummed paper)

fold up one
corner for beak

Pig

Cut a large circle (1) and a quarter circle (2) of pink gummed paper. Cut the quarter circle in two as shown and stick to the back of the full circle as ears. The full circle forms the face. Add eyes and snout (3), and stick to the cracker.

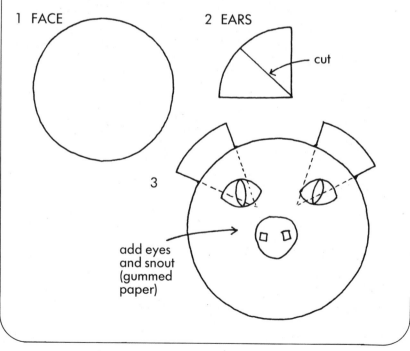

1 FACE

2 EARS

cut

3

add eyes
and snout
(gummed
paper)

Dog

Fold a square of gummed paper along the diagonal AB (1). Fold B under at DE (2 and 3). Turn, and fold tips of ears. Add eyes, nose and whiskers from gummed paper (4), and attach to the cracker.

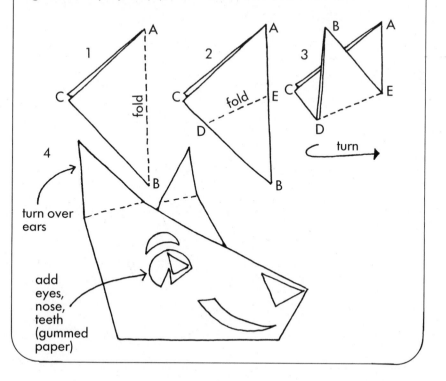

Cat

Fold a square of gummed paper along the diagonal AB (1). Fold A and B down to C (2). Fold up ears at DE and EF. Fold C up to form chin (3). Turn, and add eyes, nose and whiskers from gummed paper (4).

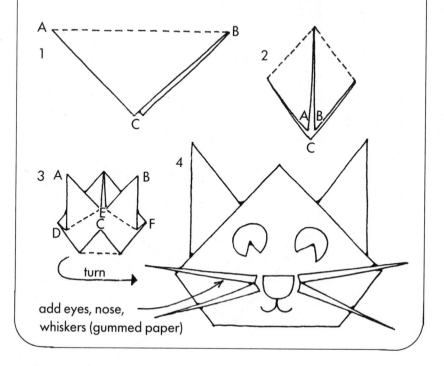

53

Other lands, other ages . . .

Advent crown

Age range
Five plus.

Group size
Small groups.

What you need
Cake base or tin tray,
4 nightlight candles,
2 oranges,
Plasticine,
foil,
evergreen sprigs.

What to do
The Advent crowns popular in Scandinavian countries
include four candles. The first is lit on the first Sunday in
Advent. The second is lit the following Sunday, and so on up
to Christmas Eve.

The traditional crown is suspended, but this design is for a
table display. It can be made on a cake base or a tray for
mobility. Cover the base with tin foil and arrange the
Plasticine in thick wads as shown. Cut two oranges in half
and scoop out the flesh. Position the orange halves at the
cardinal points and place a nightlight candle in each one.
Press holly, fir or ivy into the wads of Plasticine, and decorate
as you wish. Light the candles at suitable moments before the
end of the Christmas term.

orange

nightlight

foil

Plasticine

tray

evergreens

55

Christmons

Age range
Five plus.

Group size
Individuals or
small groups.

What you need
Card or
polystyrene,
thread,
scissors,
and a selection of
sequins, beads,
tinsel, glitter,
wire, dress pins,
braid scraps,
metallic paper,
pipe cleaners,
foil etc.

What to do

On pages 120–126 you will find designs representing early Christian symbols: crosses, fishes, chi-rho, alpha and omega, etc. In the United States they are sometimes referred to as Christmons (Christian monograms) and have for some years been used as tree ornaments.

The decorations can be made to range in height from 10 cm to 30 cm. Younger children can make them from card, adding coloured or metallic paper, or glitter embellishments. Older children might like to experiment with materials such as polystyrene shapes. Sequins and beads can be attached with pins, and scraps of braid or tinsel attached with pins or glue. Simple linear designs can be made from beads threaded on to pipe cleaners or florists' wire. The first Christmons were made in white and gold. White is the liturgical colour for Christmas, representing the purity of Jesus, whilst gold symbolises his majesty and glory.

Christmons exercise children's handicraft skills and at the same time provide a discussion topic for pupils. Make simple cards to clarify the meaning of the designs.

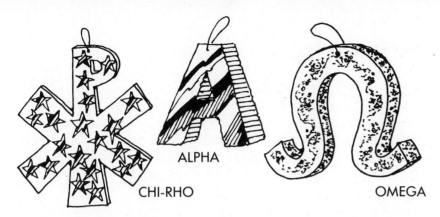

ALPHA

CHI-RHO

OMEGA

Chi-rho: This is pronounced 'kye-ro': *chi* and *rho* are the first two letters of the Greek word for Christ (Χριστος). The two letters combined were adopted as a symbol by early Christians.

Alpha and omega: These are the first and last letters of the Greek alphabet, and were taken by early Christians as a symbol of God the Father – the beginning and end of all things.

GREEK CROSS

CROWN

LATIN CROSS

CELTIC CROSS

Crosses: Symbols of Christ's crucifixion which became the most common motif of the Christian church.

Crowns: Symbols of kingship. Christ is often represented as a king in the Bible and in medieval art.

Fishes: An early symbol of Christian baptism often scratched on the walls of the catacombs. Fishes with a basket of bread are a symbol of the Eucharist.

FISH AND BREAD

DOVE

LAMB

The dove: A symbol of the Holy Ghost, reflecting the words of John the Baptist. The dove released by Noah is also a symbol of peace and good tidings, and has been adopted as a symbol of peace in modern times.

The lamb: This represents the Son of God. The lamb was a sacrificial animal in many ancient religions of the Near East, and was taken by Christians as a symbol of Christ's sacrifice. A lamb carrying a banner of victory represents the risen Christ.

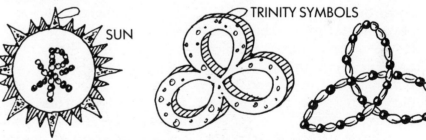

SUN

TRINITY SYMBOLS

The sun: A symbol of truth and light in Christianity and many other religions.

Symbols of the Trinity: The concept of the Trinity defied naturalistic representation, so the early Christian church often portrayed it in abstract patterns.

A Christingle

Age range
Five plus.

Group size
Individuals.

What you need
Orange or apple,
4 pieces of wood,
dried fruit,
ears of corn,
evergreen leaves,
small candle,
candle-holder,
dress pins,
glitter dust (optional).

What to do
The Christingle has very ancient origins: the Romans celebrated the end of the old year and the coming of the new with similar symbols of abundance and fruitfulness. However it has special significance for Christians. The orange or apple represents the world. The three pieces of wood symbolise the Trinity, and the fruit, corn and holly the fruits of the world. The candle represents Jesus as the light of the world.

To make a Christingle push three pieces of wood into the base of the fruit to act as legs, like a tripod. The remaining piece of wood is pushed into the side to act as a handle. The candle can be pushed into the fruit directly, or a cake candle-holder can be used instead. Make some holes in the fruit and insert the leaves and ears of corn. Finally, fix the dried fruit in position with dress pins and dust with glitter.

Collage from Poland

Age range
Five plus.

Group size
Individuals.

What you need
Card for
mounting work,
coloured
gummed paper,
sharp scissors,
adhesive.

What to do
For hundreds of years people in Poland have been making brightly coloured paper cut-outs. The design is usually based on natural objects such as flowers or birds: a cockerel is one of the most popular subjects. Each area of Poland has its own style. Some use a single piece of paper folded in half to make a symmetrical design. Others use one layer stuck upon another.

The designs make ideal Christmas cards or decorations. Cut a basic design from your first piece of gummed paper. Stick it on to the white mounting card, and then build up the picture by sticking on other layers. Do not attempt a realistic picture: achieve your effect by using bright colours and intricate cutting.

Lithuanian straw ornaments

Age range
Seven plus.

Group size
Individuals.

What you need
12 drinking straws or real straw,
strong thread,
large-eyed needle.

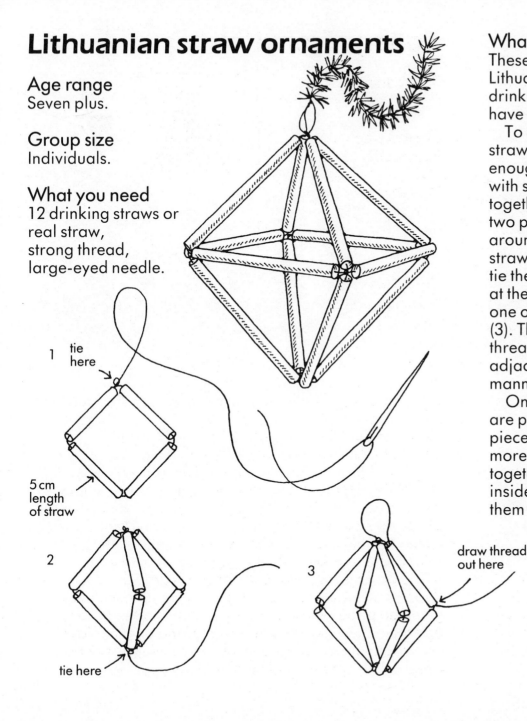

1 tie here

5 cm length of straw

2 tie here

3 draw thread out here

4 here next

thread around here

What to do
These geometric ornaments were originally made in Lithuania. The people used wheat or rye straw, but today drinking straws provide an easier alternative. If you do have access to real straw, however, experiment with that.

To make a basic square, you will need twelve pieces of straw each about 5 cm long. Thread a large needle with enough strong thread to pass through these twelve straws with some to spare. First thread four pieces of straw together and tie as shown (1). Now thread on a further two pieces of straw, and wind the thread several times around the bottom, ie between middle two pieces of straw already tied (2). Add two more pieces of straw, and tie these at the top. There should now be four straws tied at the top, and four at the bottom. Put the needle through one of the straws at the top and come out at the middle (3). Thread on another piece of straw and bring the thread around several times between the next two adjacent straws (4). Add the last three straws in the same manner. Bring the thread to the top and make a loop.

Once this basic square is mastered many variations are possible. Experiment with making the eight vertical pieces longer than the four horizontal pieces. Try adding more sides, or combining several different designs together. One might be hung above another, or perhaps inside another. Keep them as single units, or combine them to make a large mobile.

Medieval pomanders

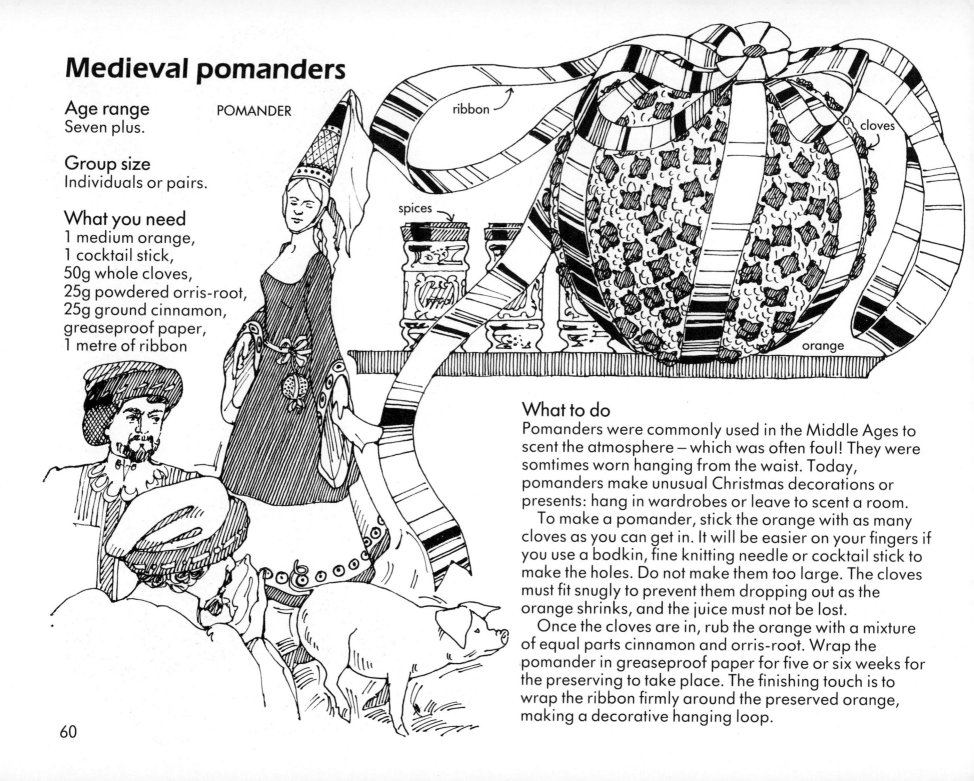

Age range
Seven plus.

Group size
Individuals or pairs.

What you need
1 medium orange,
1 cocktail stick,
50g whole cloves,
25g powdered orris-root,
25g ground cinnamon,
greaseproof paper,
1 metre of ribbon

POMANDER

ribbon

spices

cloves

orange

What to do

Pomanders were commonly used in the Middle Ages to scent the atmosphere – which was often foul! They were somtimes worn hanging from the waist. Today, pomanders make unusual Christmas decorations or presents: hang in wardrobes or leave to scent a room.

To make a pomander, stick the orange with as many cloves as you can get in. It will be easier on your fingers if you use a bodkin, fine knitting needle or cocktail stick to make the holes. Do not make them too large. The cloves must fit snugly to prevent them dropping out as the orange shrinks, and the juice must not be lost.

Once the cloves are in, rub the orange with a mixture of equal parts cinnamon and orris-root. Wrap the pomander in greaseproof paper for five or six weeks for the preserving to take place. The finishing touch is to wrap the ribbon firmly around the preserved orange, making a decorative hanging loop.

German prune man

Age range
Seven plus.

Group size
Small groups.

What you need
Wood or polystyrene
block, wire,
pipe cleaner,
fig,
walnut,
prunes and raisins,
scraps of fabric,
yarn,
felt tips.

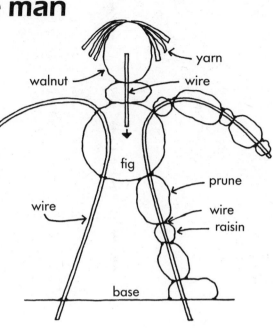

PRUNE MAN

What to do
Some German families buy these traditional figurines
whilst others make them for themselves. The prune
man or woman is made from dried fruits and nuts,
and attached to a wooden board. It is dressed in a
little jacket.

To make the figure, cut two pieces of wire and bend
them as shown. Fix the ends into a base of polystyrene or
wood. The dried fruit is pushed on to the wire. A fig
makes a good body shape, and prunes and raisins are
ideal for the legs and arms. A bent pipe cleaner will serve
as a shepherd's crook. A third wire inserted into the fig
supports a raisin neck and a walnut head. Add hair of
yarn and mark the facial features on the walnut with a felt
tip. Add any clothing you wish, using scraps of fabric.

Mexican *piñata*

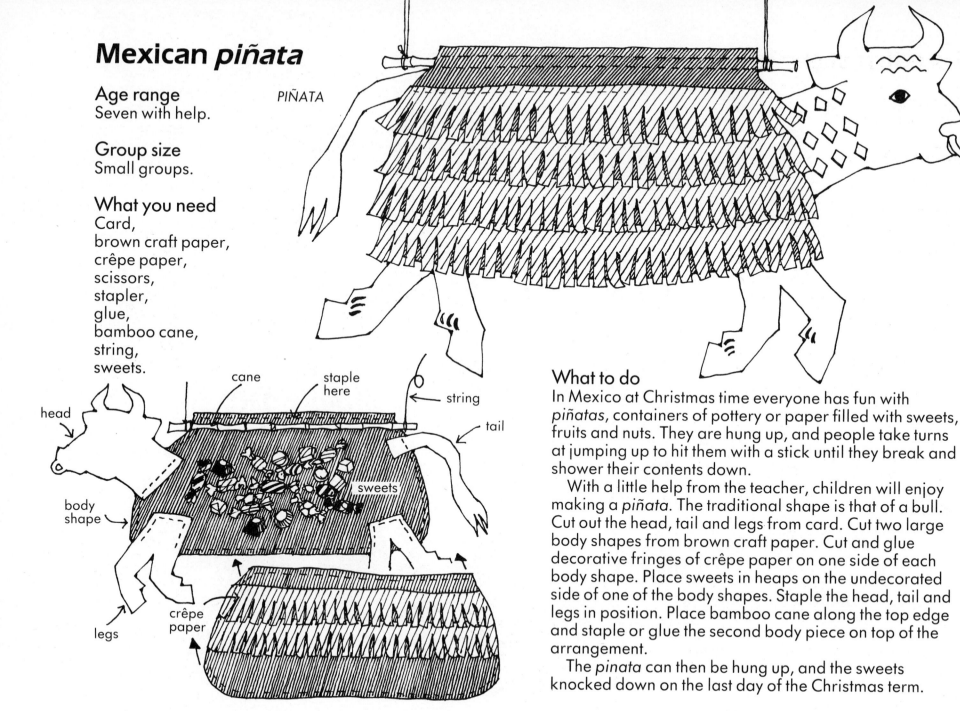

PIÑATA

Age range
Seven with help.

Group size
Small groups.

What you need
Card,
brown craft paper,
crêpe paper,
scissors,
stapler,
glue,
bamboo cane,
string,
sweets.

cane

staple here

string

tail

head

body shape

sweets

legs

crêpe paper

What to do

In Mexico at Christmas time everyone has fun with *piñatas*, containers of pottery or paper filled with sweets, fruits and nuts. They are hung up, and people take turns at jumping up to hit them with a stick until they break and shower their contents down.

With a little help from the teacher, children will enjoy making a *piñata*. The traditional shape is that of a bull. Cut out the head, tail and legs from card. Cut two large body shapes from brown craft paper. Cut and glue decorative fringes of crêpe paper on one side of each body shape. Place sweets in heaps on the undecorated side of one of the body shapes. Staple the head, tail and legs in position. Place bamboo cane along the top edge and staple or glue the second body piece on top of the arrangement.

The *pinata* can then be hung up, and the sweets knocked down on the last day of the Christmas term.

Swedish stars 1

Age range
Seven plus.

Group size
Individuals.

What you need
7 clothes pegs,
paint
(red, silver or gold),
glue.

What to do
Take the springs off seven clothes pegs and glue them back to back as shown in (1). Then glue seven pairs together to form a star (2). Finally, paint the star. Red, gold and silver are the colours traditionally used for these decorations in Sweden.

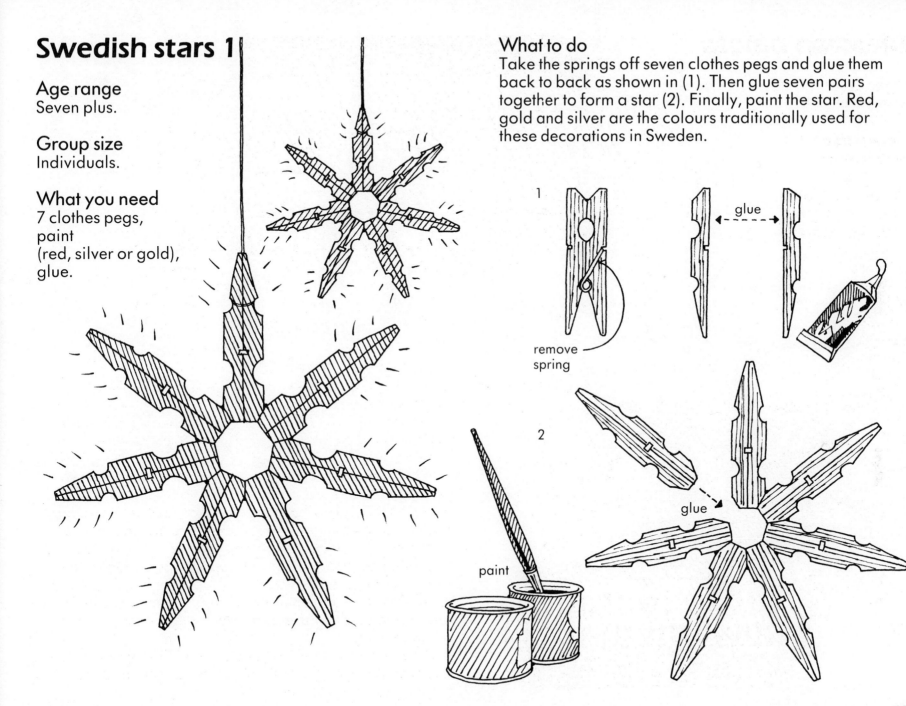

1

remove
spring

glue

2

paint

glue

Swedish stars 2

Age range
Nine plus.

Group size
Individuals.

What you need
2 drinking straws,
sticky tape or glue,
red wool.

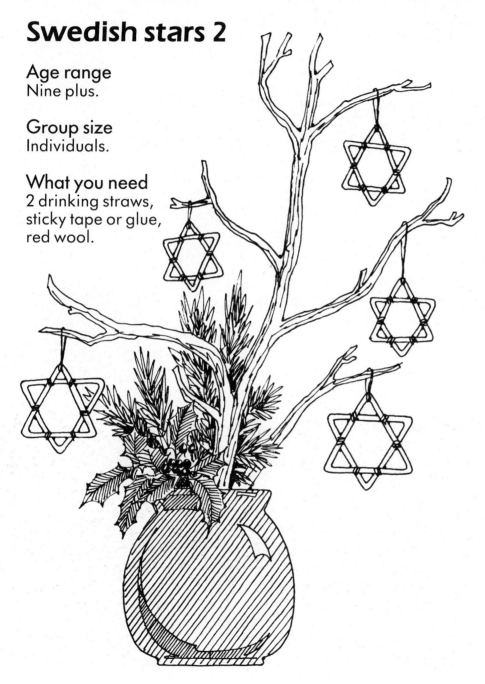

What to do

In Sweden these stars are traditionally made from real straw, but drinking straws work well and are easier to use in the classroom. Make two straw triangles, in which two of the corners are bends, and the third is secured by sticky tape or glue (1). Put one triangle on top of the other to make a star and tie them together where they cross (2). In Sweden red wool is used for the ties. Finally, add a loop from which the star can be hung.

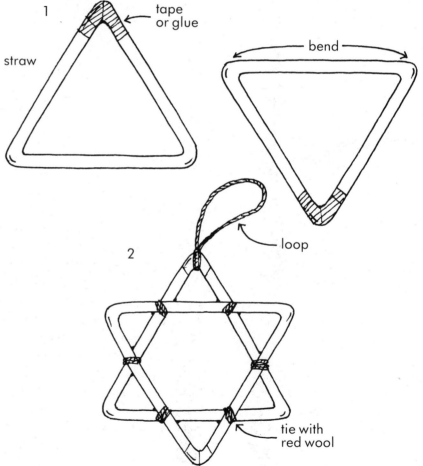

A kissing ring

Age range
Nine plus.

Group size
Small groups.

What you need
2 wire coat hangers,
fuse wire
or other thin wire,
tinsel,
ribbons,
mistletoe, holly,
ivy and evergreens.

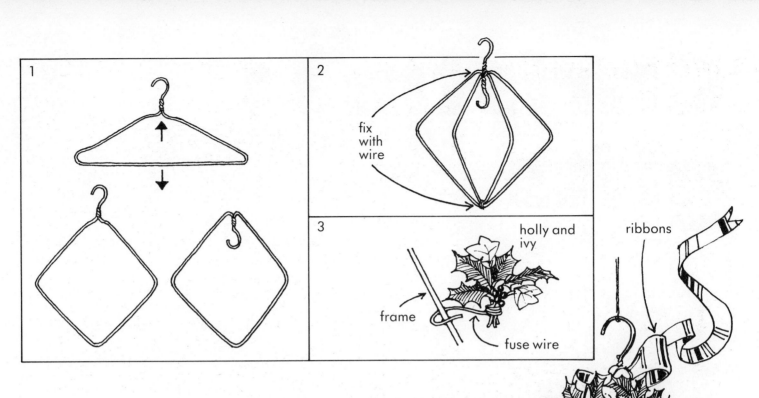

What to do
Before Christmas trees were introduced into Britain, the focal point of the decorations was the kissing ring or mistletoe bough. The mistletoe was sacred to the Druids of Celtic Britain, and continued to be revered in Christian times as a plant of peace. Kissing under the mistletoe is a sign of friendship.

To make a kissing ring, pull out two wire coat hangers so that they form a diamond shape. Bend one hook downwards to hang the mistletoe from, and the other upwards to hang the whole arrangement from. Fix the two hangers firmly together with wire. Bind small bunches of holly, ivy or other evergreen with fuse wire, leaving enough free to wind around the framework. Cover the frame well. Wrap round some tinsel to help cover the wire. Hang a bunch of mistletoe in the centre. Finally, add ribbon streamers to the top and bottom.

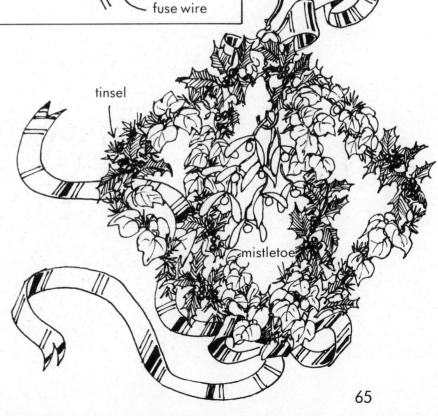

65

Christmas gifts

Snowman parcel

Age range
Five plus.

Group size
Individuals.

What you need
White fabric,
elastic band,
thin white card,
lollypop stick,
felt scraps,
glue.

What to do
Cut a large white circle from the white fabric. Place the gift – sweets, say, or some bath salts – in the centre (1). Gather the fabric round it. Secure with an elastic band (2). Cut a piece of white card (3), and decorate it with scraps of felt to make a snowman's face: carrot nose, black teeth and eyes, and a hat (4). Glue an old lollypop stick to the back of the head shape (5). Push it through the neck of the bundle to make a snowman (6).

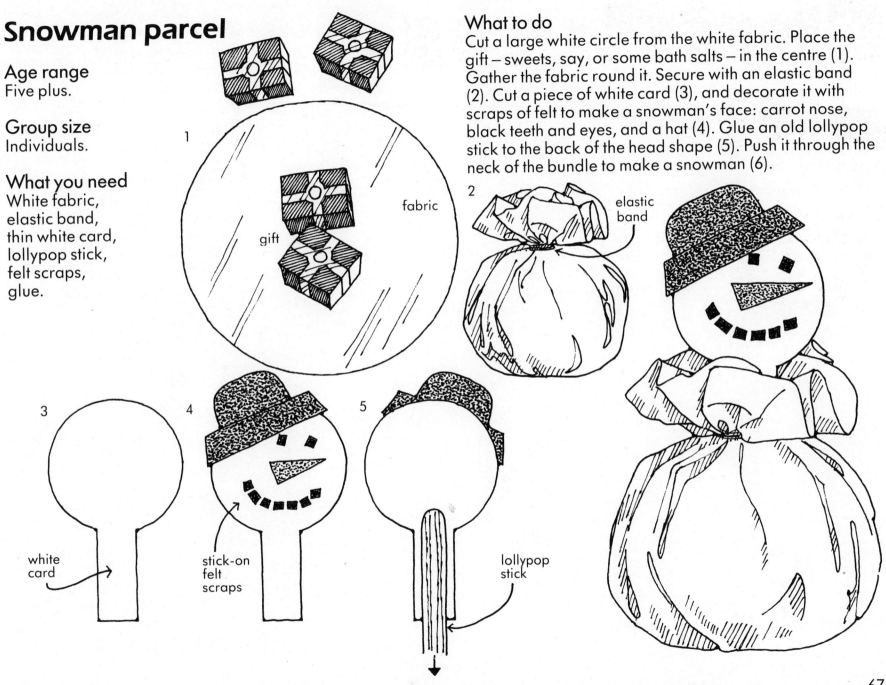

67

Santa spectacle case

Age range
Six plus.

Group size
Individuals.

What you need
Scissors,
felt (red),
felt scraps,
needle and thread,
PVA adhesive (optional).

What to do
A felt spectacle case makes an ideal small gift for
Christmas. Cut two pieces of felt approximately
10×20 cm (1). Round off the corners (2). Decorate one
piece of felt with a face so that it looks like Father
Christmas. Sew or stick on the shapes (3). Then stitch both
pieces together, leaving one end open (4).

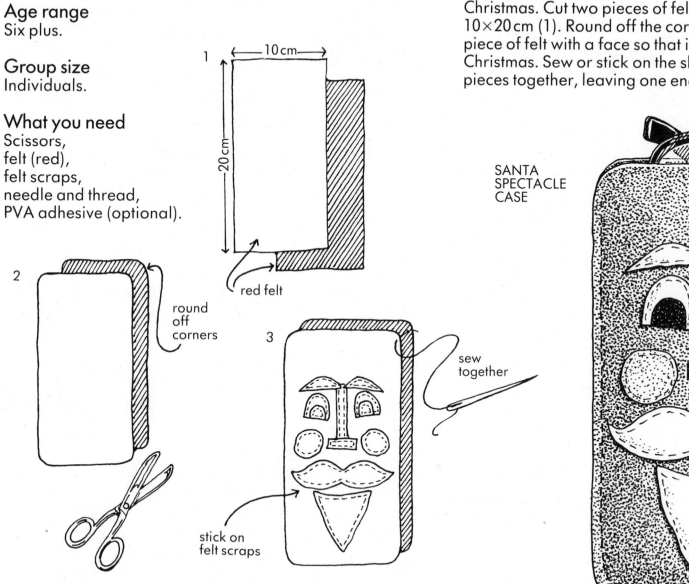

SANTA
SPECTACLE
CASE

1   10 cm
20 cm
red felt

2   round
off
corners

3   sew
together
stick on
felt scraps

Crown pincushion

Age range
Seven plus.

Group size
Individuals.

What you need
Top of an aerosol can,
cotton wool,
felt,
adhesive,
scissors,
sticky tape,
pins,
sequins or felt scraps
(optional decoration),
PVA adhesive.

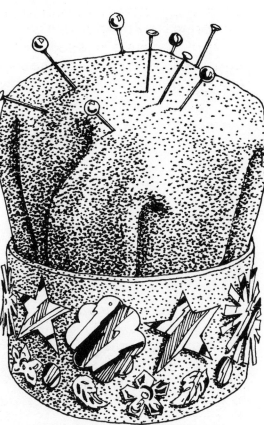

What to do
Put cotton wool in the can lid. Cut a circle of felt large
enough to go over the padding material (say 16 cm in
diameter) (1). Fix it using sticky tape (2). Cut a strip of felt
approximately 3 cm deep, and long enough to go around
the lid. This can be decorated with sequins or scraps of
felt as you wish, and stuck firmly over the sticky tape with
PVA adhesive. Finally, add a few pins to finish the
cushion (3).

The result is an attractive gift which the child can give
to a relative or friend.

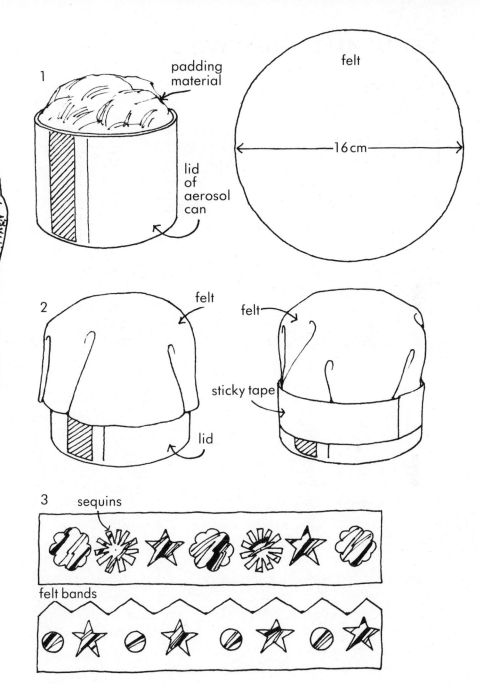

Christmas flowers

Age range
Seven plus.

Group size
Individuals.

What you need
Scissors,
card,
felt (red and green),
sequins,
plant stick,
adhesive,
cup (paper or polystyrene),
Plasticine or
plaster of Paris.

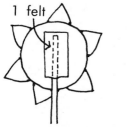

What to do
An artificial flower is an unusual Christmas gift. Cut out a
circle of card about 12 cm in diameter. Cover both sides
with green felt. Cut out six large petals and one small
circle from red felt. Stick the six petals on to the large
circle, and stick the small felt circle over the centre.
Decorate with sequins. Attach the plant stick with a strip
of felt as shown in (1). Make two leaves and glue on (2).
Decorate a paper or polystyrene cup. Fix the flower
firmly in this 'pot' using Plasticine or plaster of Paris.

Cracker brooch

Age range
Eight plus.

Group size
Individuals.

What you need
Scissors,
felt scraps,
safety pin,
sequins (optional),
adhesive.

What to do
To make this small seasonal gift, cut two rectangles of
brightly coloured felt. The first should be about 5×7 cm,
the second about 3×5 cm. Take the larger rectangle and
fringe both ends. Roll the felt and stick down the edge.
Decorate the smaller rectangle with tiny scraps or
sequins. When the first roll has dried, wrap the smaller
piece of felt around it and stick it down. Finish the brooch
by fixing a safety pin to the back.

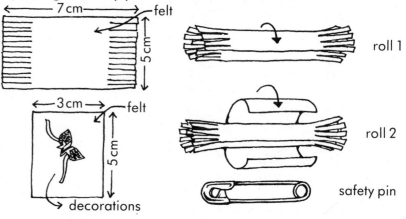

Christmas envelopes

Age range
Seven plus.

Group size
Individuals.

What you need
Paper,
scissors,
ruler,
pencil,
glue.

What to do
If you have made one of the cards in this book, you may like to make a special envelope for it. This enables you to choose its size and colour. When you are measuring, allow for the envelope to be slightly larger than your card. It's a good idea to use your card as a template. Lay it out on the paper and mark around it. Remove the card and mark in the design (1). Cut out, and score the fold lines. Finally, fold A over B; fold and stick C and D on top (2). E is tucked in (3).

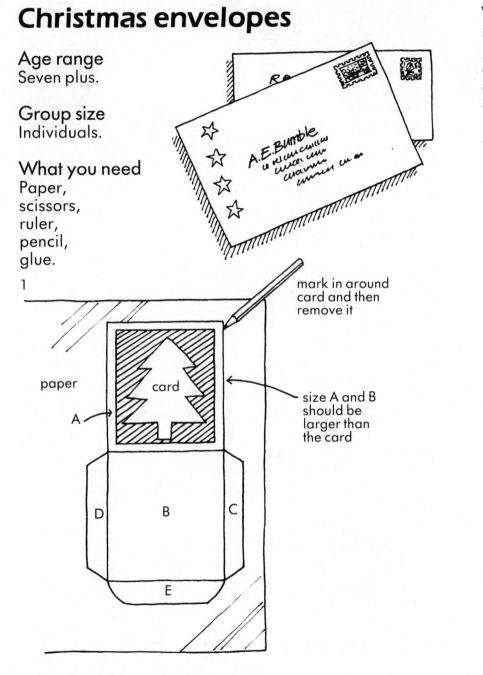

1

mark in around card and then remove it

paper

card

A

size A and B should be larger than the card

D   B   C

E

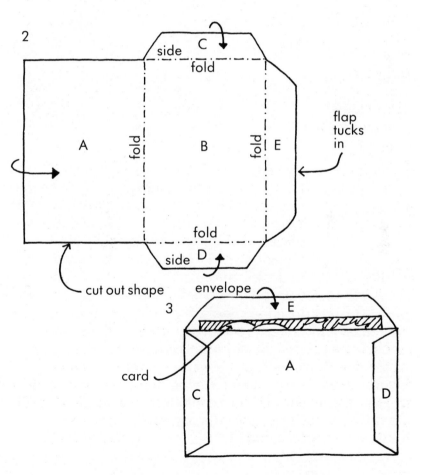

2

side C
fold

A   fold   B   fold   E

flap tucks in

fold

side D

cut out shape

envelope

3

E

card

C   A   D

Wrapping paper

Age range
Nine plus.

Group size
Small groups.

What you need
White tissue paper
or newsprint,
cold water dyes
or coloured inks,
felt tips,
shallow bowls,
newspaper,
iron.

What to do
To make unusual wrapping paper for Christmas gifts,
you will need some tissue paper or newsprint: fold it into
any of the patterns shown here. Mix up small amounts of
cold water dyes or water and coloured inks in shallow
bowls. Dip the edges and corners of the folded paper
into the various colours. Wet tissue paper is extremely
fragile, so it is safest to squeeze off excess water between
sheets of newspaper. Unfold the paper very carefully
whilst still wet. Iron the sheets dry.

   An alternative method is to use felt tips. Damp the
folded paper in clean water and squeeze off excess
water between sheets of newspaper. Using water-based
felt tips draw the design on the top fold. You might have
to open the folds and repeat the design where the ink has
not fully penetrated. Finish the sheets in the same way as
for the dye bath method.

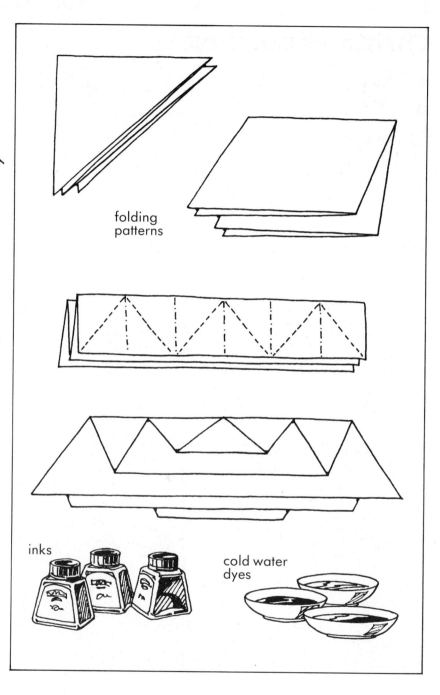

folding
patterns

inks

cold water
dyes

Christmas postbox

Age range
Nine plus.

Group size
Small groups.

What you need
Box (large, oblong),
red crêpe paper,
cotton wool,
white paper,
red and black paint,
masking tape,
newspaper,
glue,
sheet of card,
scissors.

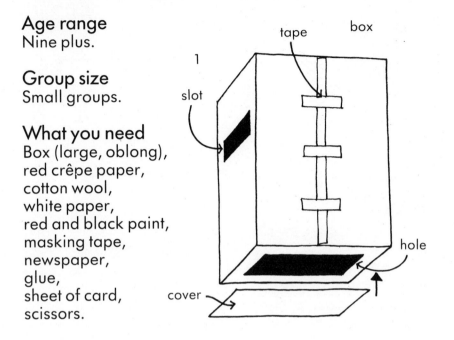

What to do
This postbox can be used for children to post each other Christmas gifts and cards. Close up all the flaps of a box and stick them down with masking tape. Stand the box on end and cut a large slot in the side without flaps (1). Cut a square hole in the base of the box. Stick the cut-out card over the hole with masking tape. This can be removed to allow parcels or cards to be collected. Paint the entire box bright red. Crumple up the newspaper and stick it on to the top of the box to give it a more rounded shape (2). Now make the front of the box into a Father Christmas. Unroll a packet of crêpe paper and place a strip over the top to act as a hood (3). Cut a large number of strips of white paper and stick these to the inside of the front of the hood so that they fall on to the top of the box, hiding the newspaper. Stick on a face, and glue more strips around the slot to form a beard. These strips could be curled (4). Stick cotton wool around the hood, neck and base, and down the front. Finally, paint in the black belt (5).

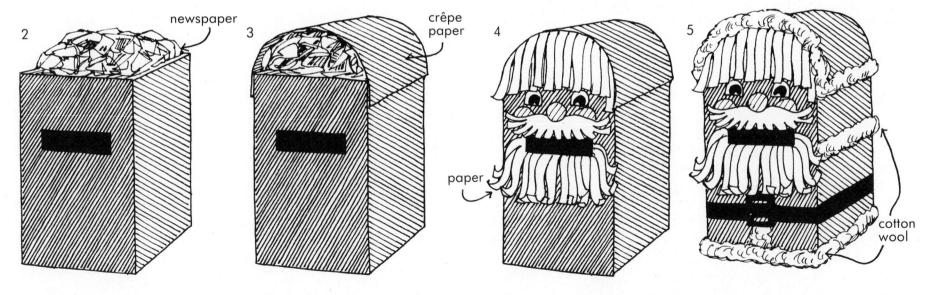

73

Party hats and fancy dress

Headbands

Age range
Five plus.

Group size
Individuals.

What you need
Strong paper or
thin card,
paper,
fabric scraps,
glue or stapler.

What to do
Cut a strip of strong paper or card at least 10 cm deep.
Measure it around the head and fix it to form a band. Cut
out a Christmas shape and decorate it. You can use a
variety of techniques such as curling, fringing, pleating,
crumpling etc. Alternatively the shape can be decorated
with scraps of fabric or coloured in. Finally, attach the
shape firmly to the band with glue or staples.

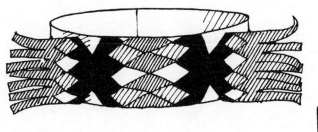

Conical hats

Age range
Five plus.

Group size
Individuals.

What you need
Thin card or
strong paper,
paper or scraps
of fabric
for trimming,
ribbon or tape
for ties,
glue or stapler.

1   card

cut

2

What to do

This party hat is a shallow cone. Cut out a section of a circle (1) and overlap the edges. Fix with glue or staples. Attach two ties (2) and decorate. Some ideas are given.

Christmas bonnets

Age range
Five plus.

Group size
Individuals.

What you need
Thin card or
strong paper,
paper or scraps
of fabric
for trimming,
ribbon or tape
for ties,
stapler.

1   card

X   X

staple

2

What to do

Bonnets, for a Dickensian Christmas, are easy to make. Cut out a shape as shown in the diagram (1). Staple the bonnet together by overlapping the spots marked X. Attach two ties (2) and decorate appropriately.

Three-in-one hat

Age range
Seven plus.

Group size
Individuals.

What you need
Paper.

What to do
With a bit of dexterity it is possible to make no less than three hats from the same piece of paper. First, fold a large sheet of paper in half (1). Fold the corners to the centre (2), and fold the top flap at the base upwards (3). Now turn the hat over and fold the side edges to the centre (4). Fold along the dotted lines and tuck inside (5).

1
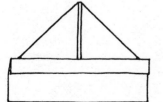

2
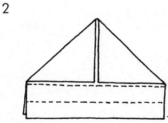

3
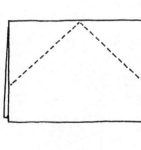

4
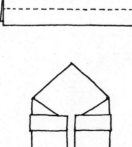

5
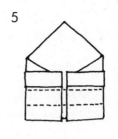

6
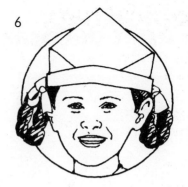

The result is a pointed hat (6)!

7
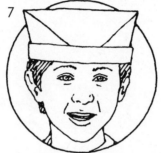

8
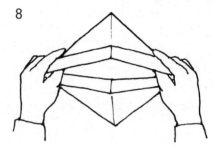

Tuck the point inside the hat band for hat two (7). Turn the hat upside down and pull apart at the centre (8). Flattened out, the hat should now look like (9). Tuck the corners into the hat band (10). Open out and you have a third hat (11)! Some ideas for decorations are shown on page 78.

9   10   11
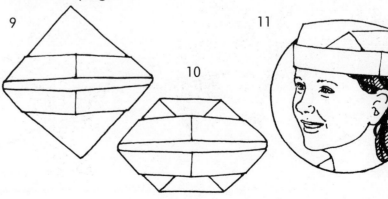

Paper decorations for hats

BOWS

STREAMERS

COCKADES

STARS

FEATHERS

FANS

Paper plate hats

Age range
Seven plus.

Group size
Individuals.

What you need
Paper plates
paint,
PVA adhesive,
scraps of fabric and
paper for decoration,
ribbon or tapes for ties,
glue or stapler.

plate

1

VICTORIANA

net braid

ties

What to do
Paper plates can be used to make a variety of pretty hats for a Christmas fancy dress party. To make hat 1 paint a plate, mixing in PVA adhesive to prevent it rubbing off when dry. Add a veil from a piece of net, attaching it with glue or staples. Finally, add some braid trimmings and the two ties. The hat will curve downwards when the ribbons are tied.

In hat 2 the rim of the plate is turned up so that the plate becomes a flat-bottomed bowl. Paint the inside with the same mixture as before. Decorate with flowers cut from paper or fabric. Attach the ribbons securely to the sides.

In hat 3 stick together two or three paper plates to make a really firm support. Decorate with fruit shapes cut from paper or fabric. Attach ribbons to the sides.

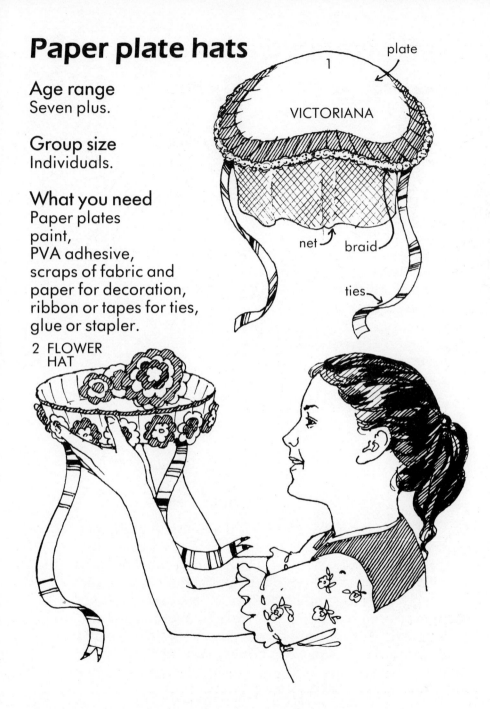

2 FLOWER HAT

3 FRUIT HAT

Cylindrical hats

Age range
Seven plus.

Group size
Individuals.

What you need
Stiff paper in a
variety of colours,
scissors,
glue and stapler.

What to do
Take a rectangle of paper long enough to be made into a
cylinder. Decorate with bold colours and flaps to give a
3D effect. Bend it around to form a cylinder. Secure with
staples or glue. The design possibilities are unlimited!

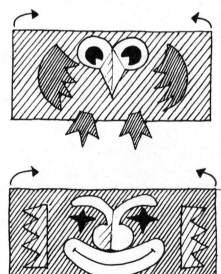

Gift-wrapped costumes

Age range
Five plus.

Group size
Individuals or groups.

What you need
Card,
tinsel,
scissors,
Christmas
wrapping paper,
crêpe paper,
foil,
gummed paper,
tissue paper,
silver paint,
small boxes,
elastic bands.

bow

ties

tag

bows

What to do
Christmas is an ideal time for dressing up and fancy
dress. The costumes suggested here can be used as
individual ideas, or collectively with groups of children
all dressed according to a common theme. In order to
keep the ideas simple, the shapes are intended to be
pinned or tied on, and the sizes can be reduced or
enlarged as required. If you have no time left at all for
preparing costumes, you could always have a 'night
before Christmas' party: the children come in their

For costume 2, neatly cover small empty boxes with gift wrapping paper and fix a length of thread to each one. Take a length of tape to make a collar and tie six to eight boxes along it. Make smaller lengths to go around the wrists. The head-dress is a large box which has been decorated. Two ties secure it under the chin.

For costume 3, cut some lengths of tinsel. Two longer lengths are required for the head-dress, one for the waist, and two short lengths for the shoes. Add a label tag as shown.

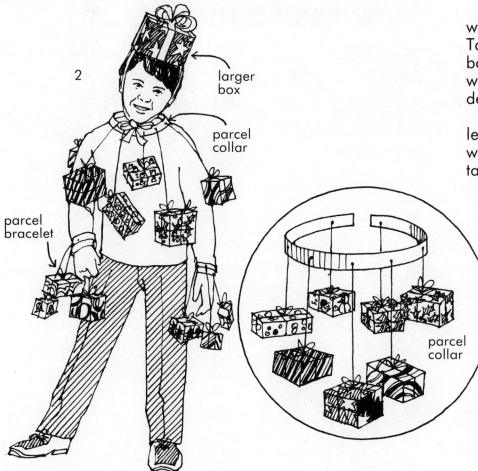

2

larger box

parcel collar

parcel bracelet

parcel collar

3

tinsel head-dress

tinsel

tag

tinsel

Merry Xmas

nightclothes and bring a letter to Father Christmas.

One good fancy dress idea is for the children to be 'gift wrapped'. For costume 1, cut strips of tissue or crêpe paper. Loop them together to form a large bow, fixed with glue or staples. Attach two long streamers securely, to act as ties. Make two smaller bows for the feet and attach them with elastic bands. Finally, make a large Christmas gift label and tie it to the wrist.

Snowstorm costume

Age range
Five plus.

Group size
Individuals or
small groups.

What you need
Paper,
scissors,
thread,
tape.

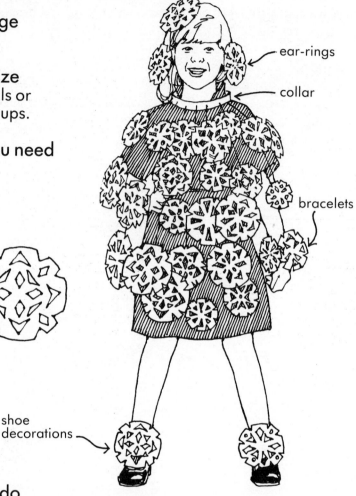

ear-rings

collar

bracelets

shoe
decorations

What to do
Make a large number of different-sized paper
snowflakes according to the pattern shown on page 43.
Attach a number of snowflakes to a series of threads. Tie
the threads to a tape to make a collar. Further snowflakes
can be attached together to make bracelets, shoes, ear-
rings, clothes etc.

Snowflake costume

Age range
Five plus.

Group size
Individuals or
small groups.

What you need
Stiff paper or
thin card,
safety pins,
glue or stapler,
scissors.

medium
snowflake
(hat)

ties

safety
pin

safety
pin

giant
snowflake

small
snowflakes
as
decoration

What to do
Cut one large and one medium-sized snowflake
according to the pattern shown on page 43. Pin the large
one to the chest. Make the medium one into a hat – glue
or staple on the ties to hold it in place. Small snowflakes
can be used to decorate the rest of the outfit.

Cracker costume

Age range
Five plus.

Group size
Individuals or small groups.

What you need
Card,
paper,
safety pins,
thread,
glue or stapler.

cracker headband

safety pin

motif

tie around waist

cracker shape

mottoes

All lit up

Age range
Five plus.

Group size
Individuals or small groups.

What you need
Card,
scissors,
glue or stapler,
thread,
safety pin.

flame headband

safety pin

tie around waist

candle shape

card candle and holder

What to do
Make a headband with a cracker motif, as shown on page 75. Cut a large cracker shape from card. Decorate it with fringed paper and a Christmas motif on the front. This covers the trunk. Attach two ties to the side, and use a safety pin for extra security. Old Christmas card mottoes can be copied on to cards and attached to wrist bands to add authenticity.

What to do
Cut out a large candle shape from card, and decorate it. Make a headband and stick on a large flame. The candle shape can be fixed with two ties around the waist, and a safety pin at the front for added security. Finally, a card candle in a holder to carry can be made.

Christmas tree costume

Age range
Five plus.

Group size
Individuals or small groups.

What you need
Green crêpe paper,
scissors,
glue or stapler,
card,
tape,
Christmas tree baubles (optional).

What to do
The Christmas tree costume is made from green crêpe paper and tape. First, make a collar (1), fixing the paper streamers to tape. Allow enough room for the head to pass through the tape collar when the ends are joined. Next, make the waistband (2), fixing streamers in the same way. This can be firmly tied around the waist. The head-dress (3) is made from a card band. Lengths of the crêpe paper are glued or stapled to the band, and a 'viewing section' cut away when the headband is in position. Christmas tree baubles can be added.

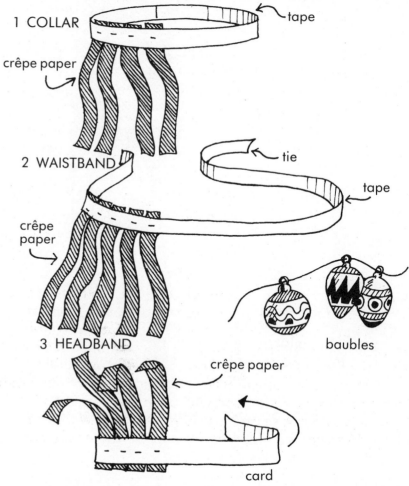

1 COLLAR

tape

crêpe paper

2 WAISTBAND

tie

tape

crêpe paper

baubles

3 HEADBAND

crêpe paper

card

All stars costume

Age range
Five plus.

Group size
Individuals or
small groups.

What you need
Scissors,
card (silver if possible),
silver foil
or silver paint,
threads,
tinsel.

HEADBAND

HEADBAND

EAR-RINGS

RING

BRACELET

What to do
To make this costume you need to cut small stars out of
card. Templates for star shapes can be found on page
112. Silver-coloured card is ideal, but if it is unavailable,
you can cover the stars with silver foil or paint them silver.
To make the collar, attach threads of various lengths to
the stars, and tie them to a length of tinsel. Tie the tinsel so
that it passes over the head with ease. Star ear-rings,
bracelets and rings can be made to wear as well. The
head-dress can be a ring of tinsel or a star headband.

Christmas plays and pageants

Heralds and minstrels

Age range
All ages.

Group size
Individuals.

Period
Medieval.

What you need
Cloth,
scissors,
ribbon,
card.

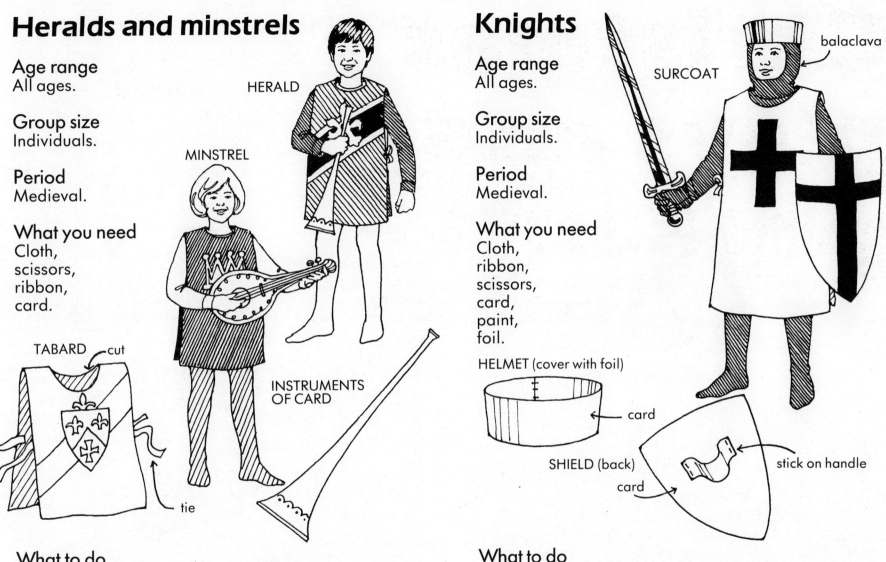

MINSTREL

HERALD

INSTRUMENTS
OF CARD

TABARD —cut

tie

Knights

Age range
All ages.

Group size
Individuals.

Period
Medieval.

What you need
Cloth,
ribbon,
scissors,
card,
paint,
foil.

SURCOAT

balaclava

HELMET (cover with foil)

card

SHIELD (back)

card

stick on handle

What to do
Cut a plain tabard as shown. No stitching is necessary as the fabric can be tied at the sides with ribbon. A crest can be stuck, painted or sewn on to the tabard. It can be worn over a plain T-shirt or sweater with tights. Musical instruments can be made from card.

What to do
The surcoat for a knight is simply a longer version of the herald's tabard. For a crusader it should be white with a red cross. The helmet can be a simple circlet of card covered in foil, worn over a balaclava helmet. Weapons and shields can be made of heavy card and painted.

Servants and maids

Age range
All ages.

Group size
Individuals or pairs.

Period
Various.

What you need
Long skirt,
apron,
scarf,
old shirt,
old tights,
belt,
purse.

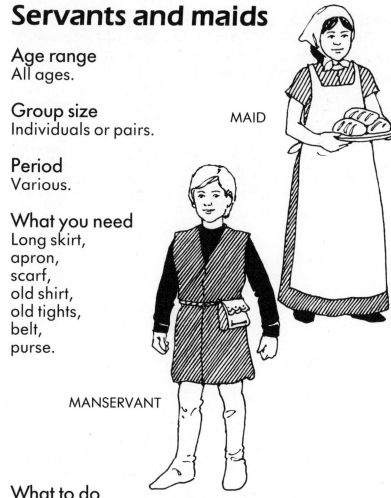

MAID

MANSERVANT

What to do
Maids and manservants appear in many Christmas pageants, and the basic clothes change little from one period to the next. For maids, a long skirt with a T-shirt or sweater is appropriate, worn with a large plain apron. The head may be swathed in a scarf or shawl. For men, a rough tunic is called for. This could be an old shirt with the collar and sleeves removed, worn over baggy tights. A purse on a belt looks good as well.

Lords and ladies

Age range
All ages.

Group size
Individuals or groups.

Period
Medieval.

What you need
Cloth,
needle and thread,
scissors,
dressing gown,
trimmings.

LADY

LORD

cut

stitch

TUNIC

What to do
Full length tunics are appropriate for both lords and ladies. Cut a hole for the neck, and stitch as shown from just above the waist to the floor. Over this tunic a gown may be worn: trim a dressing gown with fur.

Medieval headgear

Age range
All ages.

Group size
Individuals or pairs.

Period
Medieval.

What you need
Fabric, pins,
felt, cord,
scissors.

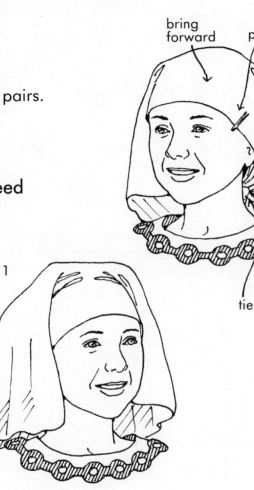

To make (2) wrap a fabric strip around the head as shown and pin it above the ears. Cut a strip of felt and secure it into a circlet. Spread the fabric over the crown and push the felt circlet on firmly.

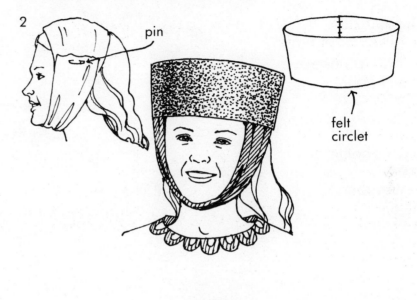

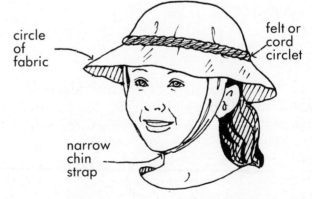

What to do
To make the head-dress in (1), take a rectangle of fabric and pull it across the forehead. Pin the cloth at both sides with a hairpin. Tie or pin the bottom corners behind the head, and then bring the fullness of the cloth forward to hide the pins.

To make (3) wrap a narrow strip of fabric around the chin and secure as in (2). Now place a circle of fabric over the head and secure it with felt or cord.

Boar's head

Stage prop

Period
Medieval.

What you need
A box about 30×23×23 cm, thick card for base (50×30 cm), plastic bottle, card, newspaper, glue, paint, varnish, tissue paper, felt scraps, an orange, gold paint, sticky tape.

What to do
A splendid centrepiece for a medieval banquet is a boar's head. Along with the kissing ring (see page 65) it was the centre of the Yuletide celebrations.

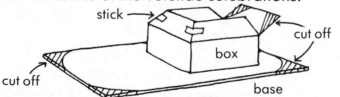

First of all, cut the base card to give it rounded corners (1). Stick on the box. Lift the flaps, and stick with tape as shown. Cut the corners as indicated.

Fix a plastic bottle as shown in (2): cut a disc of card larger than the base of the bottle and stick it on. Tape crumpled paper on to the junction of the bottle and the box. Fix on the ears cut from cardboard.

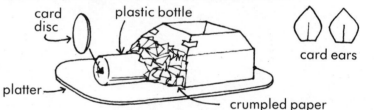

Cover and glue the head with strips of newspaper (3), and make the final layer, tissue paper. When the head is quite dry, paint and varnish it. Glue on two white tusks of card, and eyes and nostrils of felt.

Decorate with an orange and gilded evergreens.

Nativity costumes

Age range
All ages.

Group size
Individuals.

Period
Nativity.

What you need
Fabric lengths,
needle and thread,
scissors.

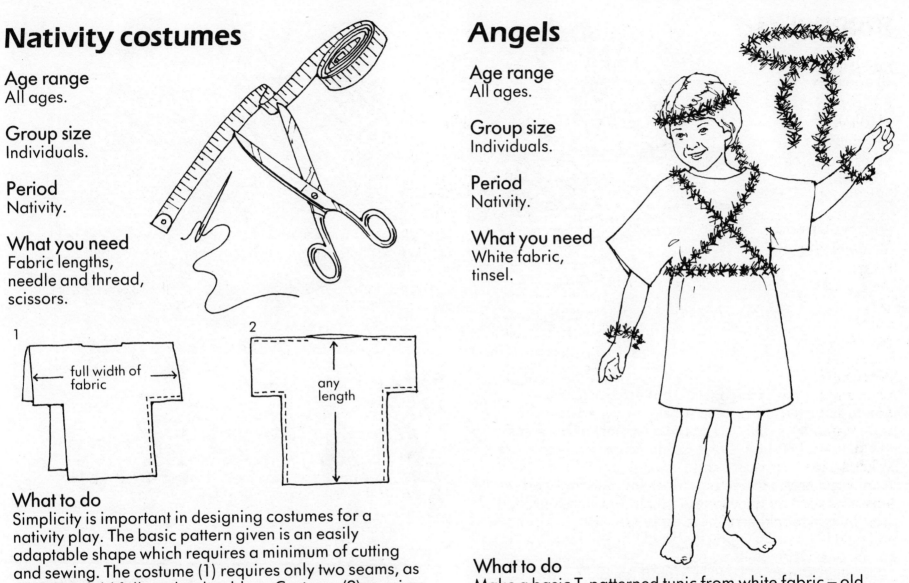

1

full width of
fabric

2

any
length

What to do
Simplicity is important in designing costumes for a
nativity play. The basic pattern given is an easily
adaptable shape which requires a minimum of cutting
and sewing. The costume (1) requires only two seams, as
the fabric fold falls at the shoulders. Costume (2) requires
four seams to be sewn. Use 91-, 114-, 137 cm wide
material and adapt the length to suit each individual
child. The neck openings can be faced with iron-on
fabric.

Angels

Age range
All ages.

Group size
Individuals.

Period
Nativity.

What you need
White fabric,
tinsel.

What to do
Make a basic T-patterned tunic from white fabric – old
sheets will do. Cross over tinsel at the front, and tie
around the waist. The headband can be tied on. Bracelets
of tinsel can also be worn. The angels can go barefoot or
wear ballet shoes.

Shepherds

Age range
All ages.

Group size
Individuals.

Period
Nativity.

What you need
Furnishing fabrics,
wools,
fur.

What to do

Again, make use of the basic T-pattern. Textured materials such as furnishing fabrics or tweeds are ideal. Keep the colours dull and muted. A variety of accessories can be used. In (1) fur fabric is slung diagonally over the shoulder. In (2) an over-jerkin is worn, belted over the tunic. It requires no seaming. Material used for head-dresses should be left ragged. An old woollen scarf or a piece of thin blanket can be adapted for a head-dress, and held in position with a fur band (3). The headband can also be worn on its own (4).

Shepherds' props might be a staff (an old broom handle) with a wire crook attached and bound with brown parcel tape; a shoulder bag, for carrying bread and cheese; a toy lamb; and lanterns. You may find that parents will supply the metal lanterns.

Innkeepers

Age range
All ages.

Group size
Individuals.

Period
Nativity.

What you need
Richer fabrics,
purses, sandals,
chains.

What to do

Again, make use of the T-pattern to design the basic
tunic. Use richer fabrics to indicate the wealth of the
innkeeper. Furnishing fabrics are ideal, and more colour
can be used than with the shepherds. An alternative to the
full length tunic is to make a layered version: a short T-
tunic may be worn over an underskirt (1). No sewing is
necessary for the underskirt, just firm pinning.
Cummerbunds with long ties can be arranged to fall in
front of the costume (2), or a rich fabric can be clasped to
one shoulder with a brooch (3).

Extra items might include neck purses or belt pouches.
Old necklaces, bangles or chains may be worn – but
don't overdo things!

Three wise men

Age range
All ages.

Group size
Individuals.

Period
Nativity.

What you need
Rich fabrics,
fur trimmings,
brooches,
sequins,
card.

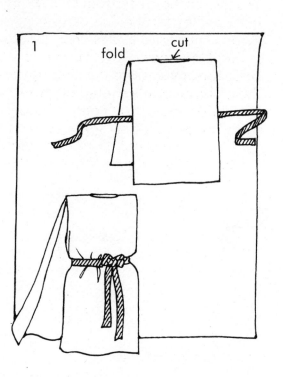

What to do
Again, use the T-pattern. The more luxurious the fabric, the better. Old velvet curtains and discarded evening dresses are a good source. Cloaks may be used, decorated with fur trimmings and sequins. An alternative costume pattern is shown in (1). The fabric needs to be at least 114 cm wide. You will need to cut a length at least twice the height of the child. Fold the fabric in half, cutting a slash at the centre for the head to go through. This can be reinforced with iron-on fabric. Fix two ties on the front section and wrap it around the body (a belt can be used instead). The back section now falls as a cloak, and can be decorated with trimmings.

The crowns can be really spectacular. A turban of rich fabric always looks good. Wrap it as in (2) and finish it off with a brooch or brightly decorated card shape on the front. The second king might wear a circlet of card (3) pointed at the front and decorated with sequins. It can be pushed down firmly over a rectangle of dark-coloured fabric which is caught under the cloak at the back. The third king might wear a tall cone of silver card (4). Decorate it with sequins and fabric.

Christmas thrones

Age range
Seven plus.

Group size
Individuals.

Period
Any time.

What you need
Cardboard,
PVA adhesive,
paints,
Christmas decorations,
chairs, tape.

What to do
Transform the classroom by making the children's chairs into special 'thrones' or use them for a play. Collect some large cardboard boxes and open them out. Tape them around the back of each chair as shown (1). This is the base for any designs the children can think of. Any paint the children apply should be mixed with PVA adhesive so that it does not rub off on clothes. Fix with tape where possible as pins and staples can damage clothes and furniture, and possibly be dangerous. Attach any kind of Christmas decorations (2).

1

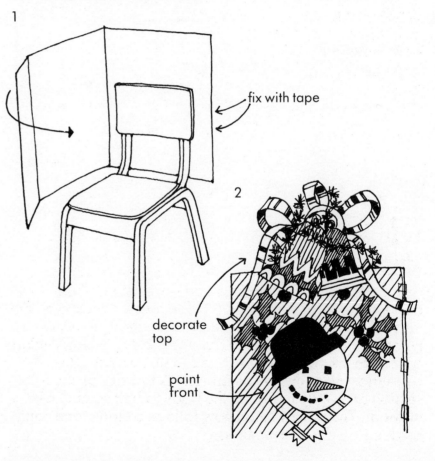

fix with tape

2

decorate top

paint front

Techniques

Scores, folds and cuts

Throughout this book you will find that scores, folds and cuts are indicated in the following way:

—·—·—·—·—·—·—·—·—·—   score

···   fold

————————————————   cut

Transferring templates

When you need to transfer a shape on to a piece of card, trace it first on to thin paper or tracing paper (1). Turn over the tracing paper and on the reverse side scribble firmly over the back of the outline with a soft pencil (2). Now turn it to the right side again, and place it on your sheet of card. Go firmly over the original tracing with a hard pencil (3).

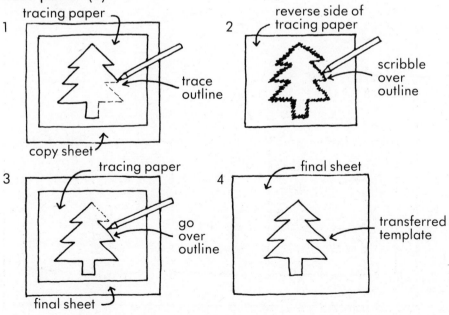

1 tracing paper
   trace outline
   copy sheet

2 reverse side of tracing paper
   scribble over outline

3 tracing paper
   go over outline
   final sheet

4 final sheet
   transferred template

Scaling up

If you want to make the shape much bigger and still keep it accurate, trace it as described, and rule a grid of squares over it. Next, rule a bigger grid with the same number of squares over your sheet of card. You might find it easier to number the squares. It should now be possible to transfer the design fairly accurately, as you will have reference points to help you.

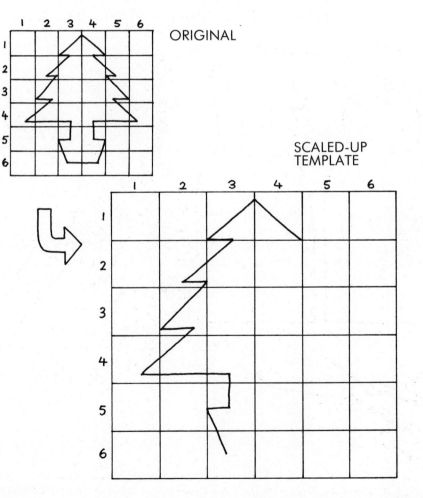

ORIGINAL

SCALED-UP TEMPLATE

Cutting shapes and stencils

Making use of a template – a cut-out shape you can draw around – makes it easier to repeat a shape. The best material to use is card. Paper is often too thin, and thick cardboard can be difficult to cut with accuracy. Old Christmas cards or a cereal box will provide templates of the right thickness. Templates are provided for many of the handicraft activities included in this book. You will find them in the section that begins on page 100.

Stencils

If you want to make a 'window' stencil, keeping the outside shape whole, the easiest way is to fold the card over and start in the middle (1). This is ideal for symmetrical shapes.

If you want an asymmetrical shape, draw the design on to the card (2) and fold (3). Cut a small hole in the paper, and then open it out. You can now continue to cut the whole shape (4).

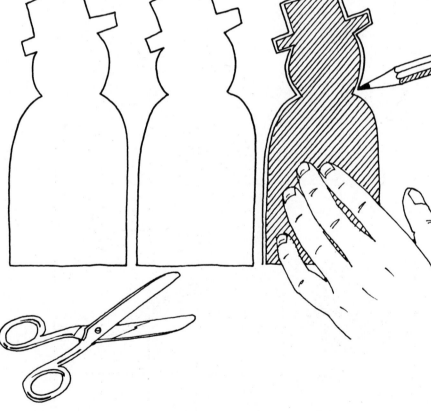

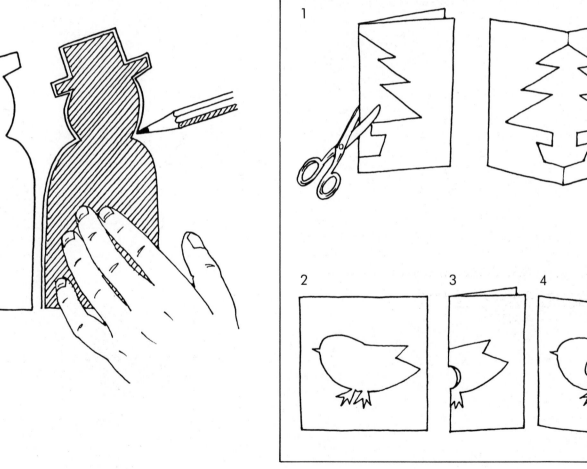

Using stencils

Using a stencil helps you to repeat a motif when painting. First of all, cut out a 'window' stencil. Place it over the paper you want to paint on and hold it firmly in place. Brushing the paint from the edge of the stencil inwards, paint over the hole in the centre of the card. Make sure that your paint is not too runny (1).

1 WINDOW STENCILS

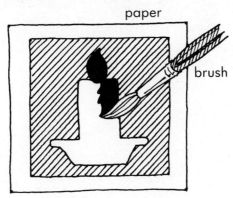

paper

brush

Alternatively, you can use a sponge and dab the paint on to the stencil. Again, make sure that the paint is not too runny (2).

2

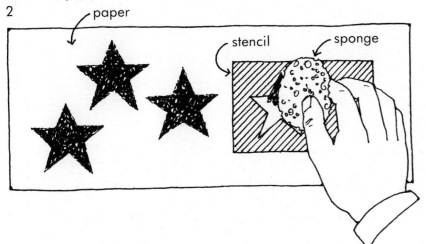

paper

stencil

sponge

Splattering is another effective way of applying paint. Use an old toothbrush. Dip it in the paint, and then pass a scraper over it as shown (3). Do not hold the paper, and make sure that you pull the scraper *towards* you – or else you too will be well and truly spattered!

3 WINDOW STENCIL

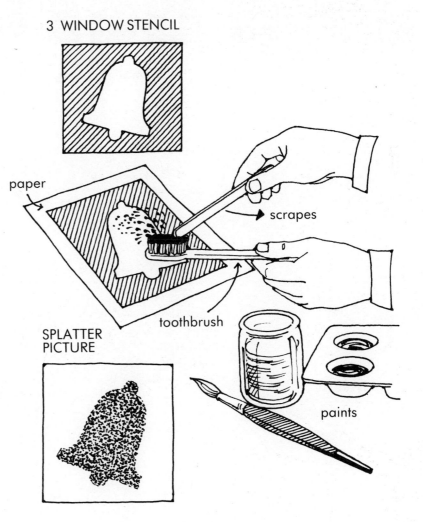

paper

scrapes

toothbrush

SPLATTER PICTURE

paints

Templates and designs

Foreign words for Christmas

Merry Christmas

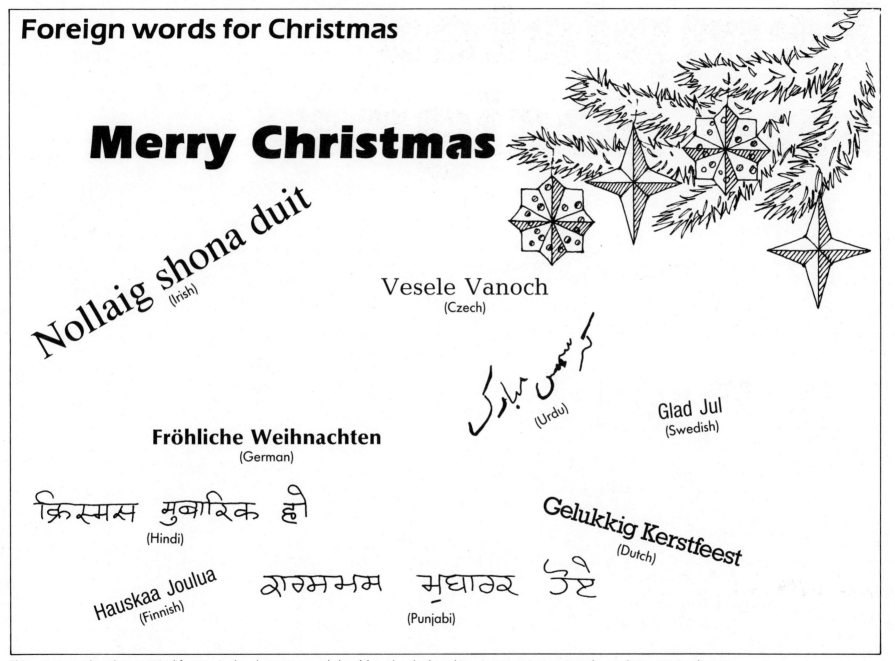

Nollaig shona duit
(Irish)

Vesele Vanoch
(Czech)

کرسمس مبارک
(Urdu)

Glad Jul
(Swedish)

Fröhliche Weihnachten
(German)

क्रिस्मस मुबारिक हो
(Hindi)

Gelukkig Kerstfeest
(Dutch)

Hauskaa Joulua
(Finnish)

ਕ੍ਰਿਸਮਸ ਮੁਬਾਰਕ ਹੋ
(Punjabi)

Foreign words for Christmas

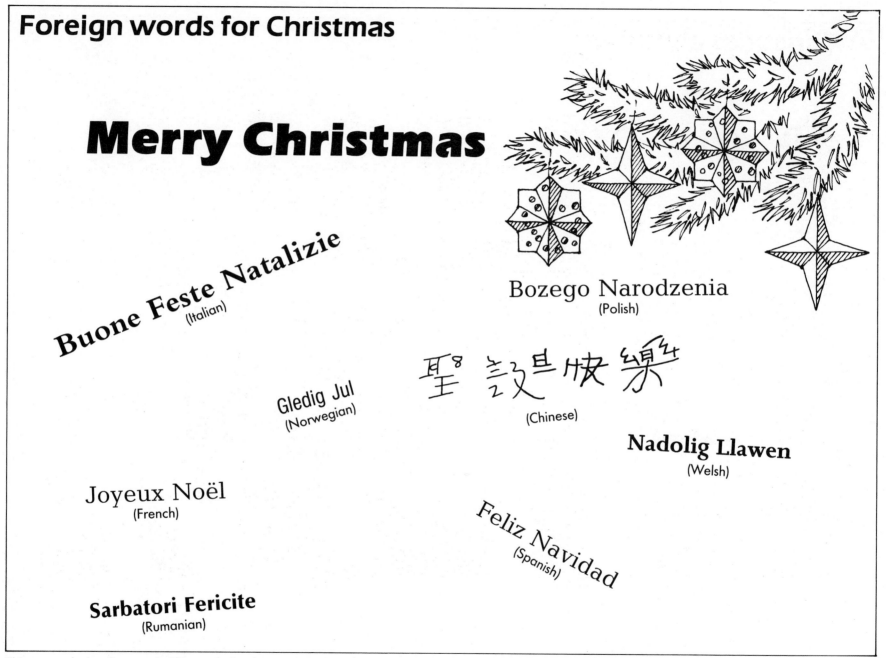

Merry Christmas

Buone Feste Natalizie
(Italian)

Bozego Narodzenia
(Polish)

Gledig Jul
(Norwegian)

聖誕快樂
(Chinese)

Nadolig Llawen
(Welsh)

Joyeux Noël
(French)

Feliz Navidad
(Spanish)

Sarbatori Fericite
(Rumanian)

A Christmas alphabet

Christmas gift alphabet

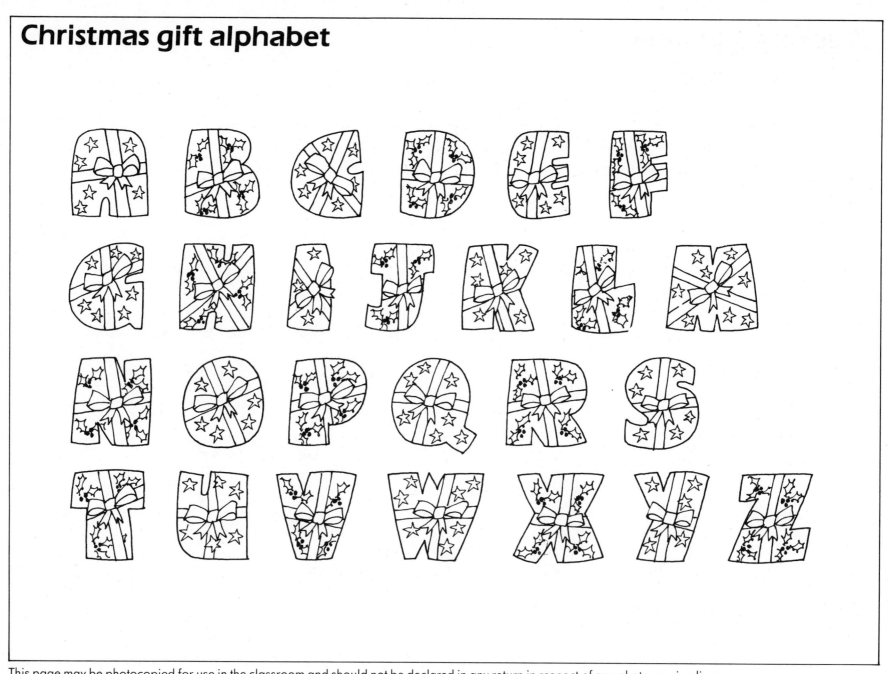

Crackers alphabet

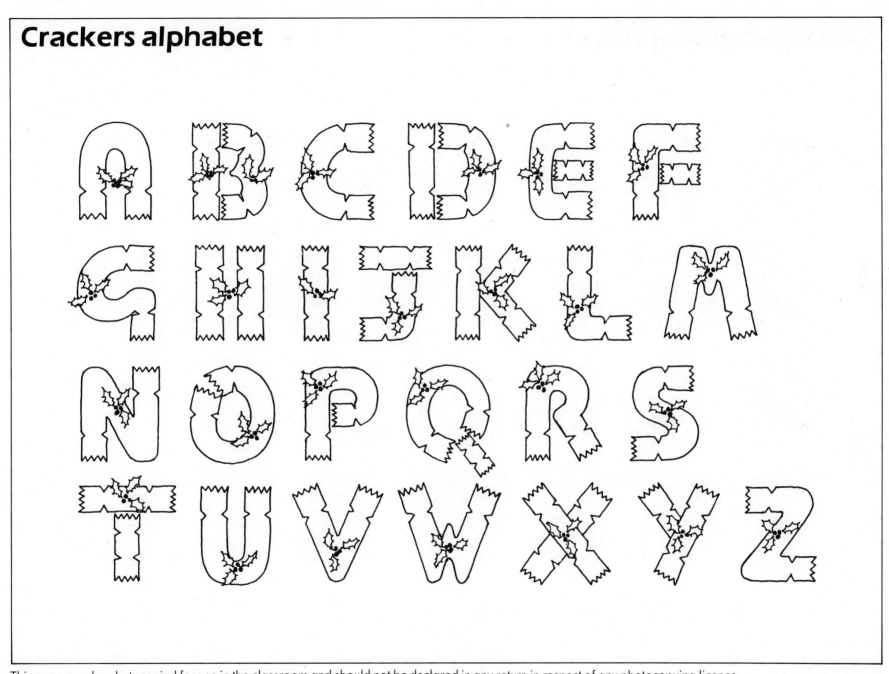

Snowman alphabet

Designs for embroidery, page 10

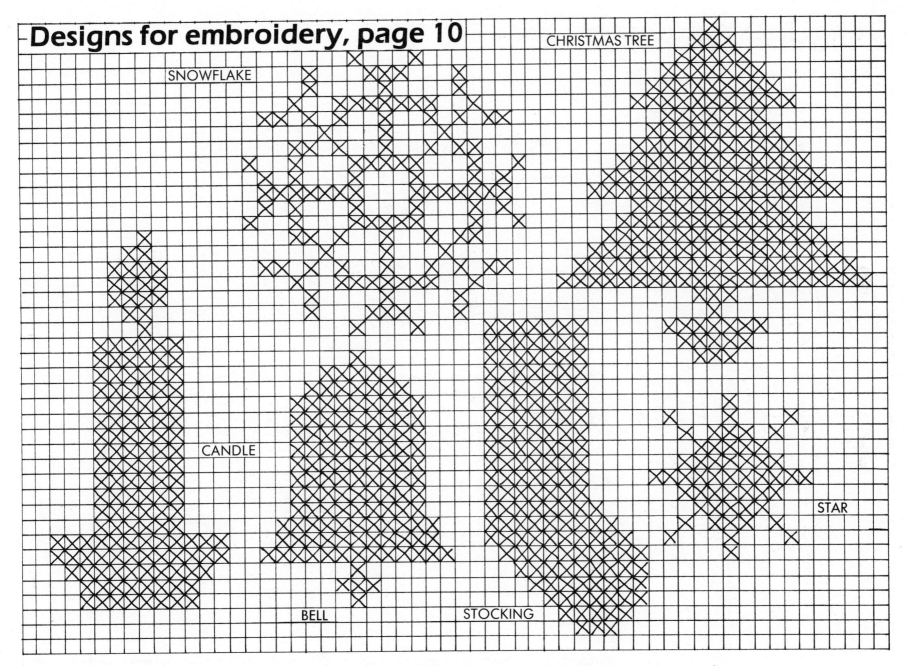

SNOWFLAKE

CHRISTMAS TREE

CANDLE

STAR

BELL

STOCKING

Stencil for splatter cards, page 11

BELL

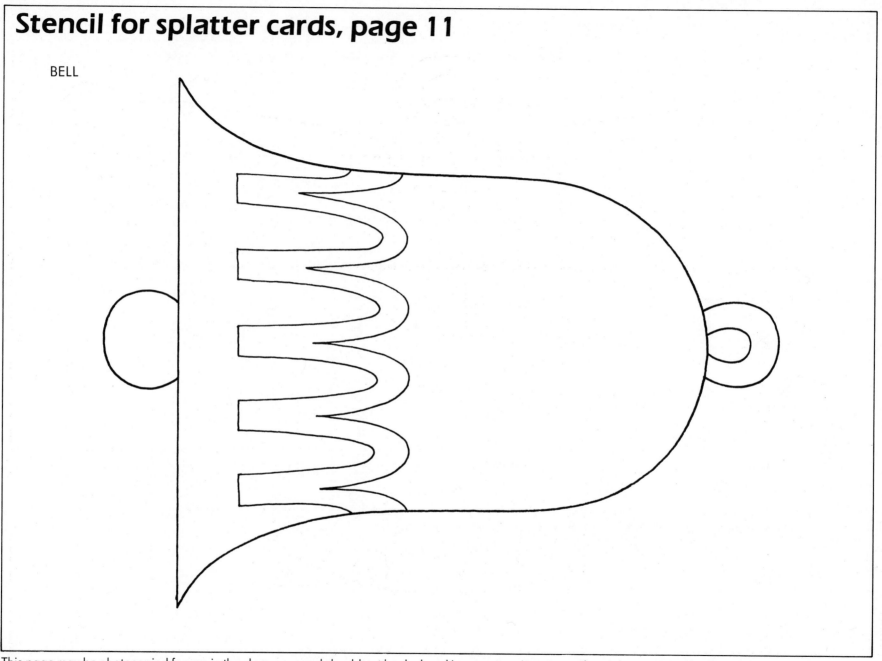

ANGEL

CHRISTMAS TREE

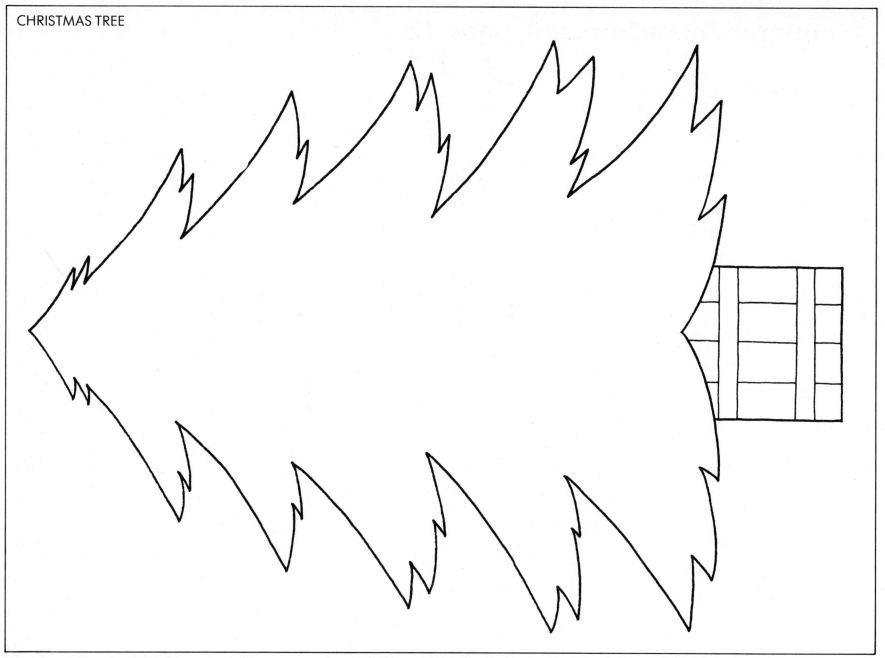

Template for cracker card, page 12

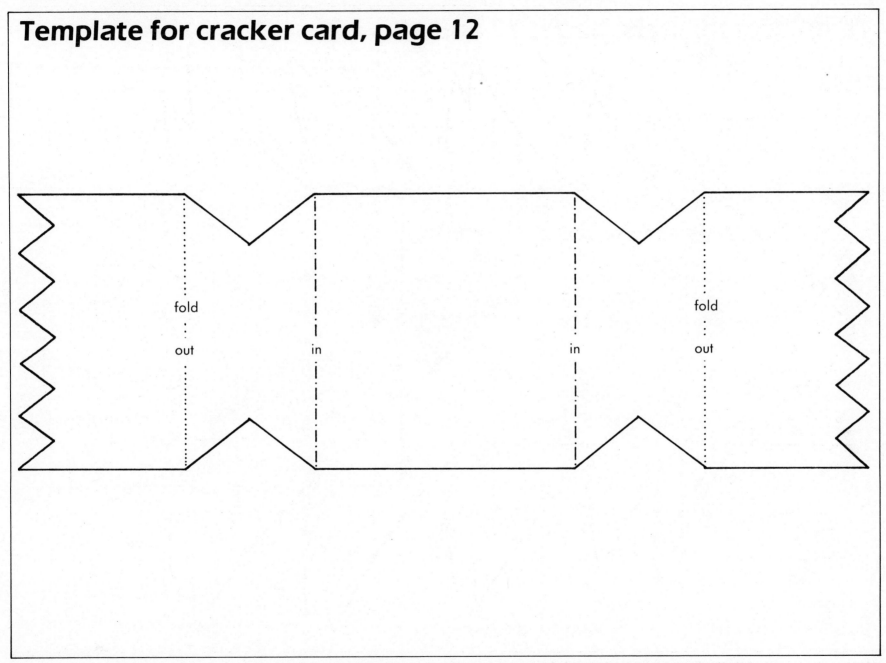

fold

out

in

in

fold

out

Templates for stars, pages 17 and 18

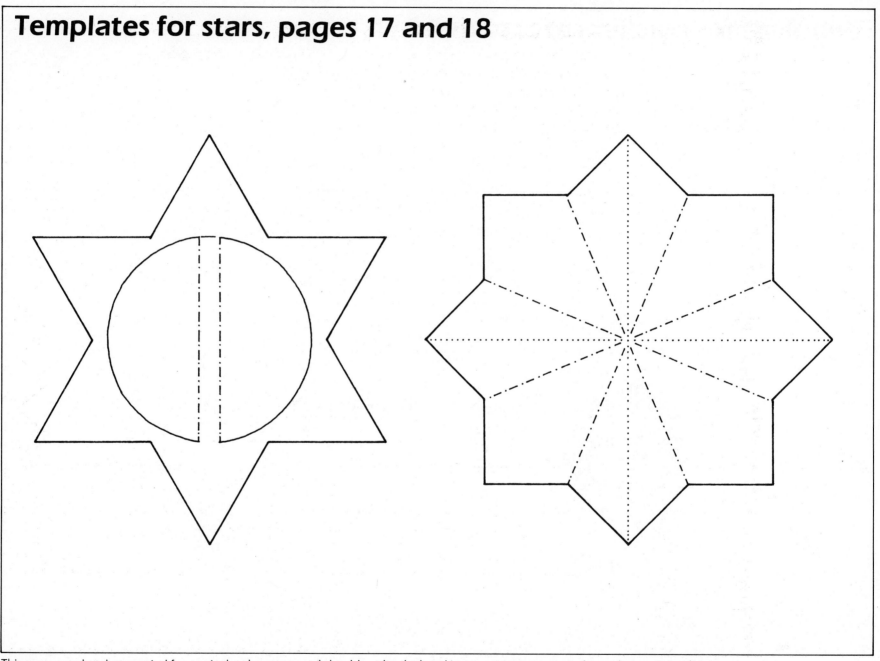

Template for 'All square for Christmas', page 20

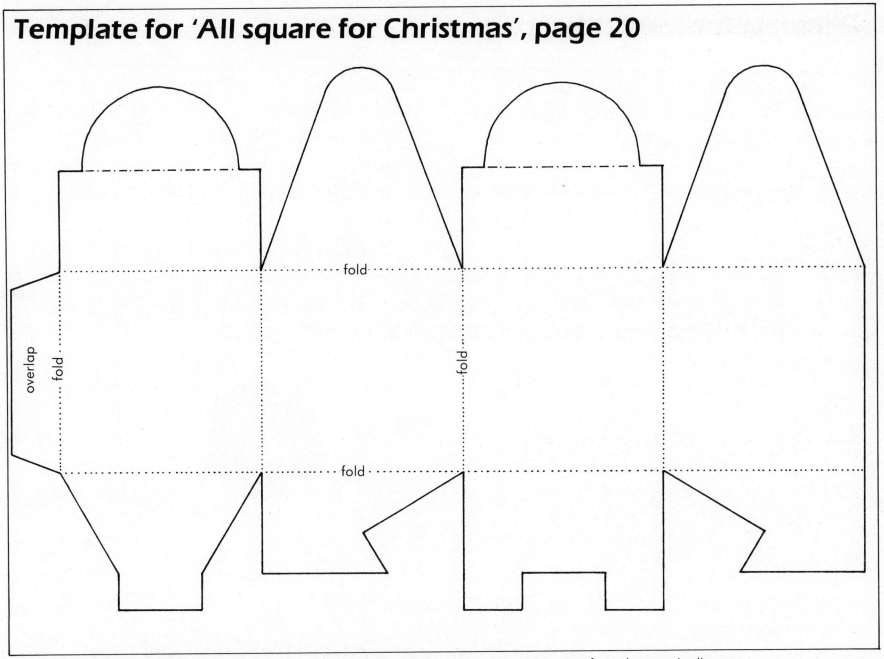

overlap

fold

fold

fold

fold

fold

Template for tree shoes, page 21

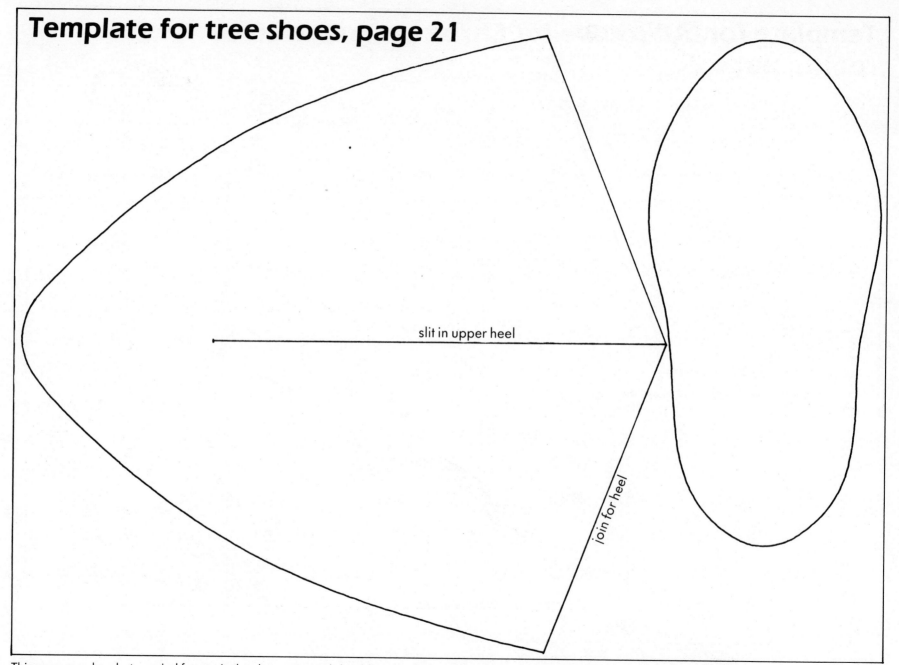

slit in upper heel

join for heel

Template for Christmas robins, page 22

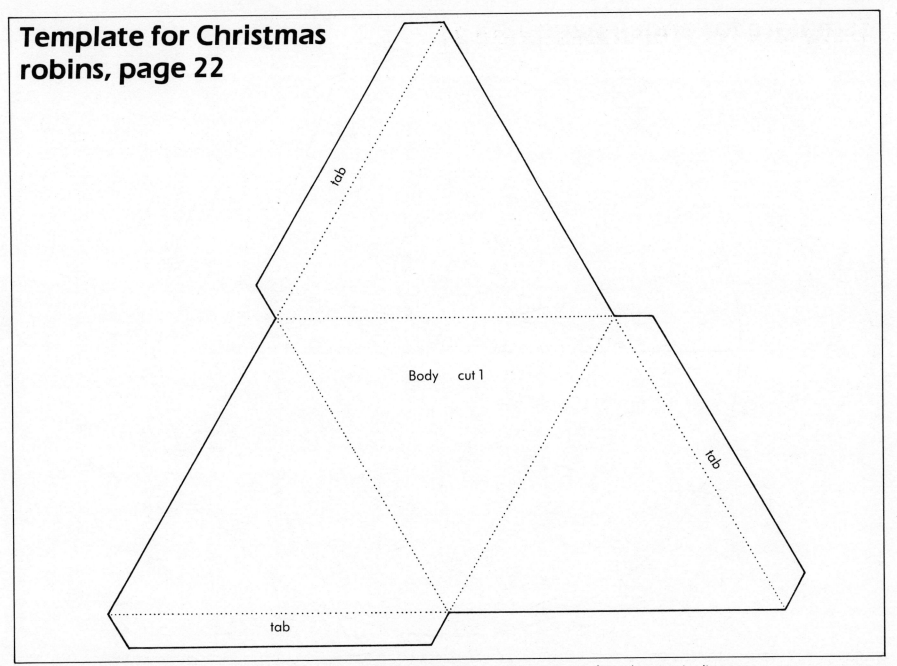

tab

tab

Body   cut 1

tab

Template for angel, page 23

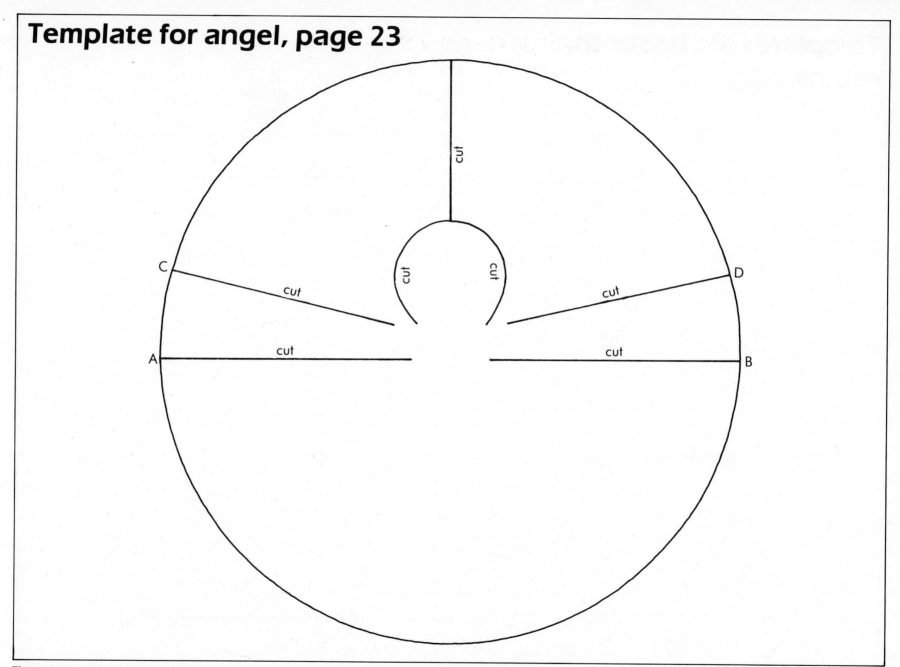

Templates for paper chains, page 29

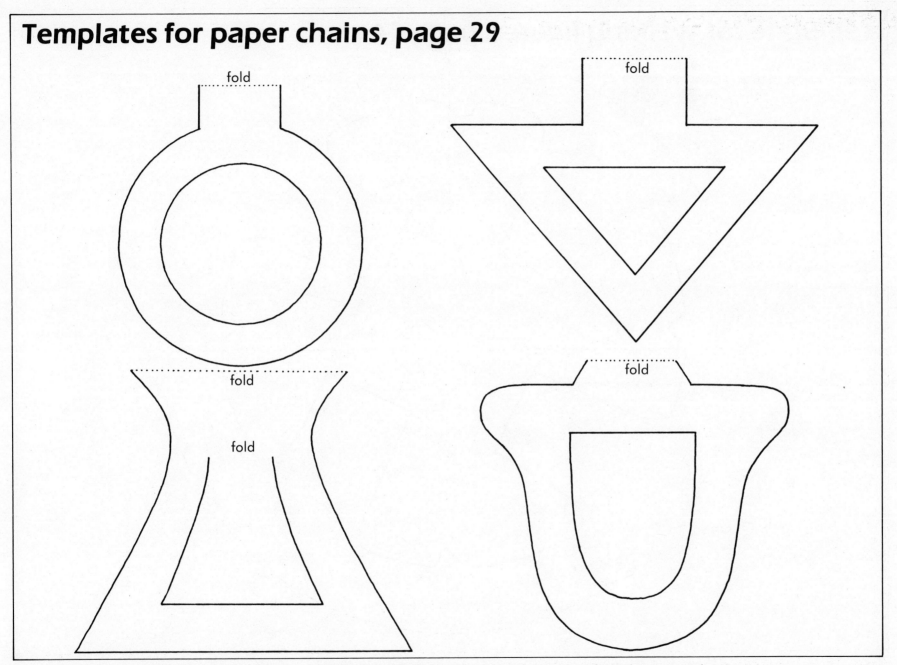

fold

fold

fold

fold

fold

Template for walking figures, page 44

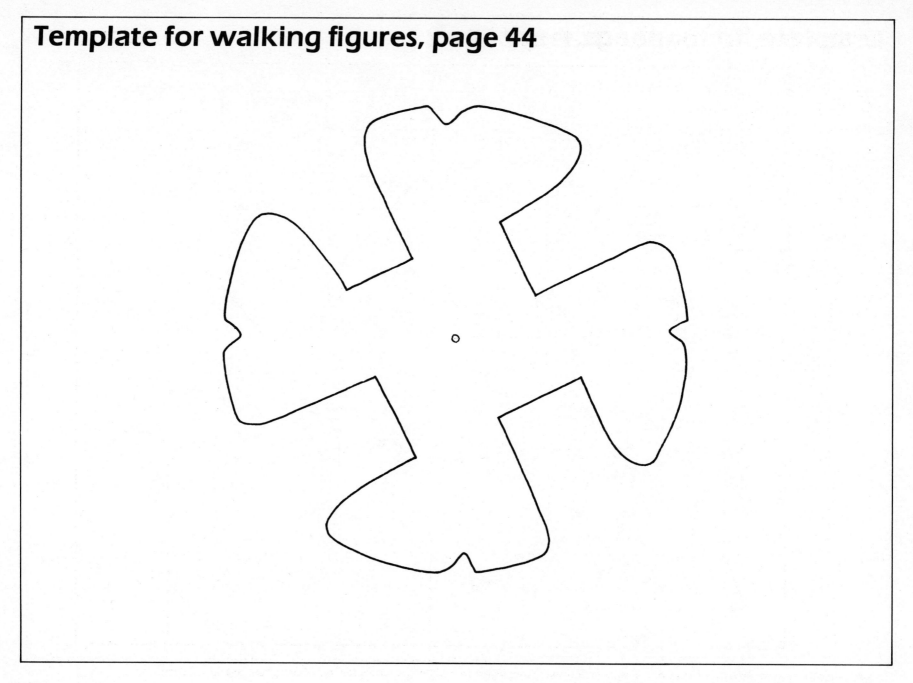

Template for minibags, page 50

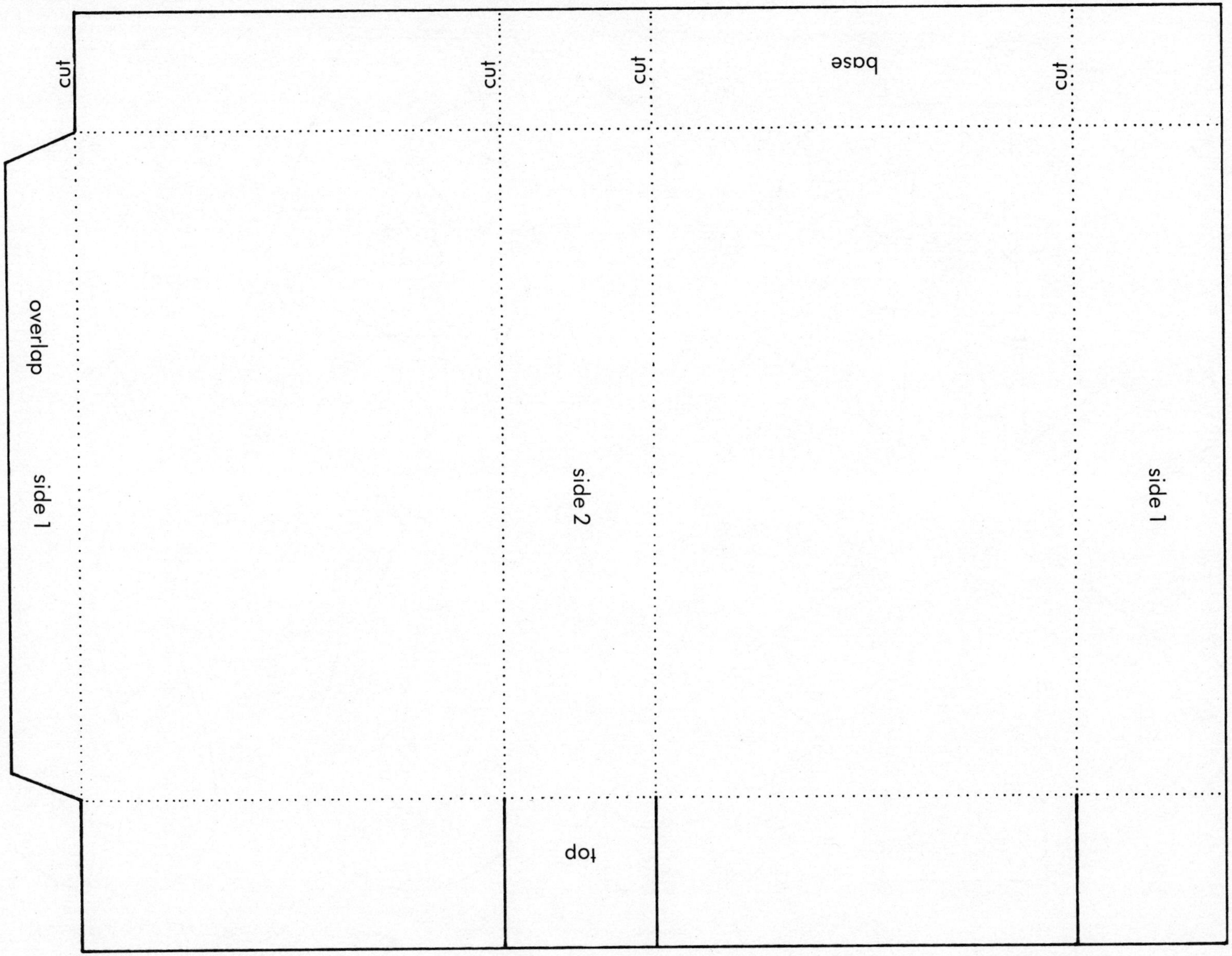

cut   cut   cut

base

cut

overlap

side 1   side 2   side 1

top

Templates for Christmons: Greek symbols, page 56

ALPHA

CHI-RHO

OMEGA

Templates for Christmons: Crosses, page 56

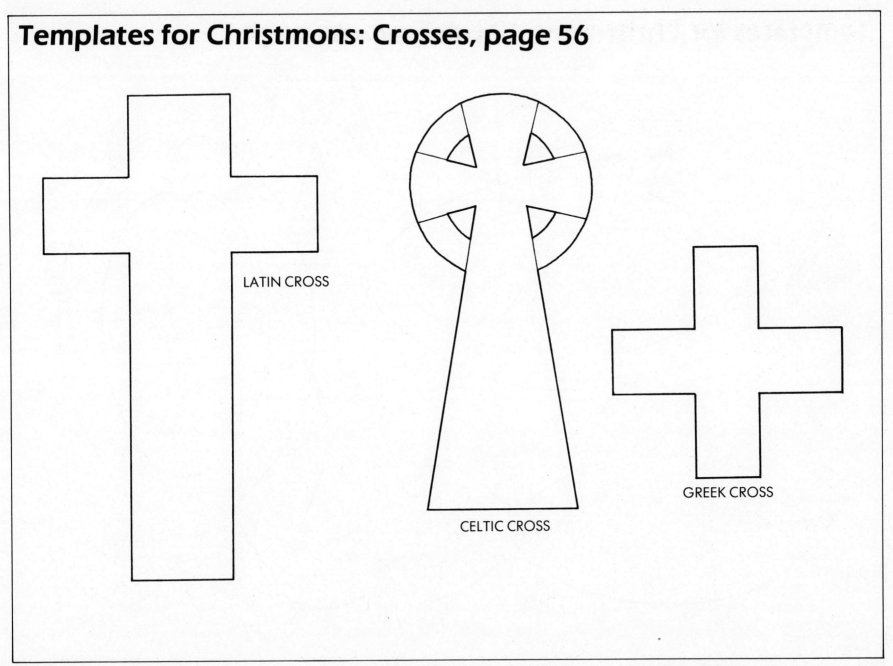

LATIN CROSS

CELTIC CROSS

GREEK CROSS

Templates for Christmons: Fishes, page 57

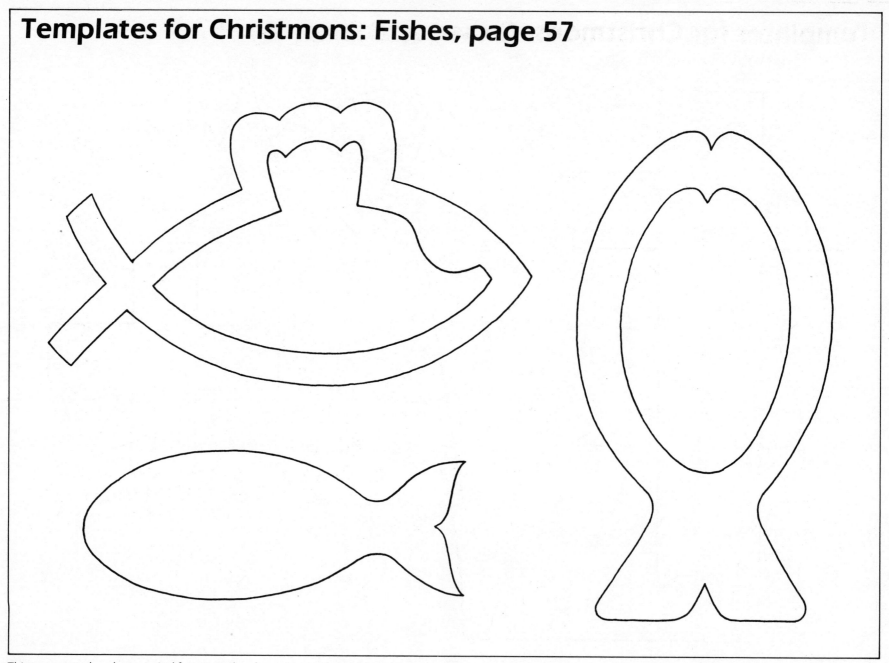

Templates for Christmons: Crown and Sun, page 57

CROWN

SUN

Templates for Christmons:
Dove, page 57

Templates for Christmons: Lamb, page 57

This page may be photocopied for use in the classroom and should not be declared in any return in respect of any photocopying licence.

Templates for Christmons: Trinity Symbols, page 57

More Christmas Bright Ideas

The first Bright Ideas for Christmas Art and Craft contained templates for the following:

Snowman,
Bell,
Five-pointed star,
Six-pointed star,
Eight-pointed star,
Angel,
Tree,
Christmas baubles,
Holly,
Candles,
Father Christmas,
Stained-glass window,
Bethlehem,
Three kings,

Shepherd,
The Holy Family,
Lamb,
Donkey,
Shapes for mobiles –
snowman, Father Christmas,
crackers, Christmas trees,
candles.
Snowflakes,
Pyramid tree,
Christmas-card stars,
Cone figures,
Tiered cone tree.

There are also tips and ideas on;

- Techniques: cutting, scoring, folding, templates, stencils and rubbing
- Christmas trees for table decorations and large Christmas trees.
- Christmas tree ornaments
- Stars for the tree-top
- Advent Calendars
- Nativity figures and cribs

Acknowledgements

The editors and publishers extend grateful thanks for the reuse of material first published in *Art & Craft* to: Anthony Hearne for 'Christmas robin'; Bob Neill for 'Christmons'; Warren Farnworth for 'Paper angel'; Margaret Geddes for 'Advent crown' and 'Kissing ring'; Ruth Hancocks for 'A four-pointed star', 'Octahedral stars', 'Peep-in octagonal star', 'Peep-in hexagonal star', 'Ladder streamers', 'Streamers from circles', 'Streamers from squares', 'Barrel lantern', 'Straight-sided lantern', 'Waisted lantern', 'Four-bar lantern', 'Inside-out lantern', 'Father Christmas lantern', 'Paper bells and balls', and 'Forwards and backwards shapes'.

Every effort has been made to trace and acknowledge contributors. If any right has been omitted, the publishers offer their apologies and will rectify this in subsequent editions following notification.